A GRAND ADVENTURE

MEMOIRS OF A MISSIONARY NUN

SISTER HELEN WARMAN, OLSH

Edited by
SALLY GODDARD

UNDERHILL BOOKS

DEDICATION

To my mother and father and my sister Jean
To the Religious men and women and the lay people I
worked with in Milne Bay
To the women, children and teachers of Papua New Guinea

———

All profits from the sale of these books will go to OLSH
projects in Papua New Guinea.

FOREWORD

SISTER MARIFE MENDOZA

Sr Helen Warman has been a Daughter of Our Lady of the Sacred Heart for sixty-five years. Since 1959 she has dedicated herself to working with and for the people of Papua New Guinea (PNG). Gifted with the ability to teach, she ministered in schools in remote areas of the country including Daio, Budoya, the Trobriand Islands and other parts of Milne Bay Province. While working as Religious Education Coordinator for Papua New Guinea and the Solomon Islands she was based for a number of years in Port Moresby, the capital city of PNG. Recognizing Sr Helen's fine contribution to education, the PNG Government conferred on her the Logohu Award.

In this book Helen invites us to meet her own family in suburban Sydney, to see the people and relationships which formed and sustained her through the years. We also see the influence on her of the Daughters of Our Lady of the Sacred Heart, whose schools Helen attended for both her primary and secondary education. Helen then transports us to Papua New Guinea and we meet so many of the people she loved and served.

To those who have lived and worked in Papua New Guinea the stories Helen relates resonate with their own experience. For those who have not visited or worked in Papua New Guinea she opens a window on the life of both the local people and the missionaries.

It is my hope that you will enjoy the pages of this book as much as I. On behalf of the Congregation I thank Sr Helen and all the Sisters who have ministered in Papua New Guinea between 1887, the year of our first arrival, and today. May their stories continue to inspire us!

— *Sr Marife Mendoza*
Congregational Leader
Daughters of Our Lady of the Sacred Heart
Rome, Italy

INTRODUCTION

DR. STELLA ADORF

The first time I met Sister Helen was at my friend Kate's pre-wedding reception in her parents' house on Prince Edward Island in Canada. Not long after my arrival and a few hellos to people known and unknown to me, an older lady, with a big smile on her face, came towards me. Sister Helen introduced herself and we talked. Always trickling into her narratives was a good portion of her great sense of humour and empathy. She shared memories of her years in Papua New Guinea and the special people she had met. I ended up sharing her room that first night because my accommodation arrangements had fallen apart.

I felt very blessed to be able to spend time with Sister Helen. Her fascination with people and things was contagious. Seeing the world through her eyes, I often wondered to myself, this must be the best life a person can live. Most intriguing was the fact that one could visit an ice cream factory with her, and enjoy tons of the sweet cream, while simultaneously having deep philosophical conversations. I was not able to remember a time I had felt so mentally intrigued and at peace with the world at the same time as in our week together back then.

Somehow, this lady of a more senior age and petite size seemed to have seen it all in life, and knew more about this world than any of us did. Sister Helen is one of the few human beings who understands this world, all of its good and its evil, and, most importantly, what to make of it all. She remains truthful to one thing: Being a force of good in this world. Her 'goodness' is, however, not missionary, not forceful, never pushing. It is simply contagious. Her whole being appears to consist of positive energy.

Sister Helen's thoughts, words and ideas seemed like a bright light to me in a sea of concerns. It remains to be said that we did not talk about religion or faith in those days, not that I remember it anyway. Her way of seeing things, of perceiving the world and the people in it, made me reflect on my perspectives and adjust. I say adjust, because she never really attempted to change anything that I thought or said or felt, but somehow I seemed to be a bit more 'back on track' after the days spent with her. Sister Helen found a way to inspire me through compassion and love and curiosity for life.

Sister Helen's story is of truth and goodness, so it does not come as an entire surprise that the idea of telling this story occurred during a time when the world struggles with a pandemic and all the worries and hardship that accompany it. Sister Helen's life is also a story of love, of faith and belief, of adventure and frontiers, of passion and determination, of so many values that matter even more during these days that we are witnessing. Now, let us meet Sister Helen!

—*Stella Adorf, PhD*
  Brussels, Belgium

ONE

MY FAMILY

AUSTRALIA 1935 - PRESENT

Family is not defined only by last names or blood: it's defined by commitment and love. It means showing up when needed most. It means having each other's backs. It means choosing to love each other even on those days when you struggle to like each other. It means never giving up on each other.
—*Dave Willis*

I WAS BORN on December 1st, 1935, the second daughter of Ernest John Warman and Eileen Bernadette Wilson, in Sydney, Australia.

MY FATHER MET my mother who was waitressing in a milk bar (similar to a soda shop) down near Central Railway. He was there alone when a group of young men arrived who made lots of noise and banged on the tables. When they left, my mother was dismissed, because the woman who owned the milk bar said my mother was the attraction for these young men.

As she walked down the street, she saw an advertisement for a waitress at another milk bar. She told the woman why she had lost her previous job. The owner said, "We'll take you on but if anything happens you'll have to go."

My mother started working and this young fellow turned up again. When Mum went over to serve him, he started to talk to her. She said, "Please don't talk to me, please go, I don't want to have anything to do with the customers. I'll lose my job."

He said, "All right."

When my mother finished work, the same man was standing outside the door and he said, "Where do you live?"

My mother said, "I live at Redfern and I catch the tram home."

He said, "I'll walk up with you."

This man was my father. He went up to the tram stop with Mum and stood beside her as she waited. A woman came up and said to Mum, "Who's that fellow?"

Mum explained, "It's alright, he's just brought me to the tram stop."

The woman said, "Are you okay?"

Mum replied, "I'm fine."

As the woman walked away, Dad asked, "What are you talking to her for?"

Mum said, "Because every time I finish work and come here, she tells me to stand beside her. She's been doing it all the time."

Dad said, "Don't you know she's Rosie, the prostitute!"

She must have seen something in Mum, because Mum would stand next to Rosie. As the fellows would walk up, Rosie would say, "Keep going! Keep going!"

Then she would put Mum on the tram to go home. Mum said, "I don't care who she is. She's looked after me all the time I've been coming here to get the tram." After that Rosie never stood beside her because Dad was there.

Dad went home and told his mother he was going to get engaged to this girl in Sydney. Then he dropped the bombshell, "She is a Catholic."

Nana said, "We don't want any of that blood in the family. Get rid of her and get one of your own."

Dad said, "No, I'm not going to get rid of her. I'm going to keep her."

Nana retorted, "I'll come down and meet the girl."

Nana invited Mum and Dad out to a restaurant. Mum had never been to a restaurant in her life and here she was going to one with her boyfriend to meet his mother. As they were having the meal, Nana ordered a cup of tea. The waitress brought the teapot and left it on the table. Nana picked up the teapot and she started to pour the tea into the cup.

Suddenly she started calling, "Waitress, waitress, come quick, come quick." Mum said she was so embarrassed because everybody in the restaurant was looking at them.

The waitress came running and said, "Madam, what's the matter?"

Nana replied, "Woman, do something, the tea has fainted." She meant the tea was really weak. Mum was sure Nana only did it to embarrass her. You know, to see if she would say, "No, Ern, you take your mother and go, I don't want either of you."

Many years later Nana used to say to Mum, "Oh, Eileen, what if he'd taken notice of me and sent you away. I would never have had you as my daughter." When Nana was dying she asked for mum to come and nurse her at home and my mother did.

Before they were married, they would spend time together on Sundays. Mum always told Dad she would never go out on a Sunday until after the 8 o'clock Mass. One day he announced "We'll leave at 8 o'clock."

Mum said, "No, I can't leave at 8 o'clock, I have to go to Mass first."

Dad promised, "I'll take you to Mass on the way."

They left at 8 o'clock and along the way they came to a church. Dad said, "Let's go into Mass here."

At the end of the Mass the priest told the congregation, "Now, after Mass today we are going to have a baptism. Anyone who wants to stay and be part of the ceremony is welcome."

Mum whispered, "Let's go because we don't know these people who are being baptized."

Dad said, "Oh no, let's stay and see them baptized."

Then the priest called out the names of the people who were to be baptized, and he called out, "Ernest Warman." Much to Mum's surprise and delight Dad was baptized. That was that! He had been attending catechism lessons to prepare for baptism for six weeks. They were married in St Peter's Catholic Church in Surrey Hills on the 16th April 1932.

My parents had 6 children but only my sister Jean and I survived. The others were all boys, affected by the Rhesus factor[1] and died shortly after they were born. I remember when we went to the Royal Hospital for Women to visit Mum. I couldn't have been any more than 4, because I had to stretch out my arm to hold my father's hand as I walked beside him. When we came out I said, "I am so angry. I am so angry with those nurses."

Dad asked, "Why are you angry? They're looking after your mother."

I said, "No. No, they're not. They gave every lady in the ward a baby but they didn't give one to my mother." My mother must have just lost a baby and they hadn't moved her out of the maternity ward.

When I was about 9, my mother's sister, Auntie Kitty, asked me if I would like to learn how to knit baby booties. I thought this was a wonderful idea. I waited for her to return with the wool and knitting needles but when I next saw Aunt Kitty and asked her about making the baby booties, she said she'd like to leave them for another time. I realized later my mother must have lost another baby.

My mother once said that God had always looked after her. I asked her about the four babies she had lost and she said, "Yes, yes I lost them but I had you and Jean." She always looked on the positive side of life.

My father began his working life on the trams as a conductor. Then he became a driver and when the buses replaced the trams, he obtained his driver's license. Eventually, he became an inspector in the city rather than in the suburb where we lived. He didn't want to be an inspector where he had worked for so many years, because that was where his friends were.

My father was a real time fanatic and I've inherited that I'm afraid. I'm dreadful. If you come to me and say 7 o'clock I'll be there at 7 o'clock and I expect you to be there at 7 o'clock — not 2 minutes past but 7 o'clock.

My mother once said to me, your father loves both of you so much. I think that I tried to be the son that he didn't have. I killed the chickens with him at Christmas time. I raked up the grass when he cut the lawn with the mower. When he cleaned the shoes and put the polish on I would shine them. At the weekends we went to football and cricket matches with him. Whatever he did I did with him.

When he was a tram conductor he wore waterproof trousers and hooked them onto buttons at his waist. These protected him from the weather as he walked along the running board on the side of the car collecting fares. When he'd come home he'd ask, "Who wants to pull off my leggings?" Jean and I would both sit down and pull off his leggings and lollies or a sweetie would fall out.

My father was quick to anger but it never lasted very long. He would blow up about something that he didn't like, go outside and then come back in as if nothing had happened. I'd watch Mum dealt with it. She'd say to us, "Don't worry. Your father gets mad, let's off steam and then is fine." I think my mother had the patience of a saint.

MY MOTHER HAD this tremendous faith. She believed. She believed in God, and she believed in Our Lord and Our Lady.

My father came to church when Jean and I were small and we made our First Holy Communion. I can remember another time he came for Mass, because the priest gave a sermon the infallibility of the Pope. After mass, Dad said, "When I went into the church I knew nothing of the infallibility of the Pope, and now I have come out of the church, I still know nothing about the infallibility of the Pope."

Mass on Sunday was the big thing. My sister and I worried about Dad because he never went to Mass on Sunday. We told Mum how worried we were that we would be in heaven one day without Dad. Mum said, "Don't worry, we'll pray and one day he'll go to Mass and he'll come to heaven with us." She never worried. She never badgered him, she never asked him, but every Sunday, from the time we were tiny, she took us to Mass.

My parents — Ern and Eileen Warman

After my father died in 1987, Mum moved to a lovely villa. It was in an area shaped like a horseshoe with houses separated by garages. Across the road lived Kate and every time my sister drove in or I would be there, Kate would come over. I would say, "Here comes that woman again." My mother explained her visits and said, "Let her come. She's never had the love in her life that we've had."

Kate came over one day and revealed that her husband, who was a Catholic, was dying. After she left, I thought I should do something. I went over to Kate's house and asked her if she would like me to find a priest to visit her husband. She thought that would be a good thing. I found a priest who took care of the husband. After the husband died, Kate came to Mum's and said, "I want to become a Catholic."

The parish priest met with her and said, "Eileen can instruct you."

Mum was astonished and replied, "There's no way. I don't know anything"

The parish priest explained, "Just teach her what you believe."

Kate became Catholic having taken Mum's instruction, and then went on to become an instructor herself.

My mother had great faith. In the Catholic church, St. Anthony is the one you pray to if you lose anything. When Mum prayed to St. Anthony, what you lost just appeared in your hand almost. I was staying with Mum and Jean came to visit. When it was time to leave, she couldn't find her car keys. We looked everywhere and couldn't find them. Mum said, "Stop worrying. Leave it to St. Anthony and we'll play a hand of euchre. "

When we'd finished, Jean stood up and said worriedly, "I just don't know where those keys are." She put her hand on top of a cupboard and there were the keys.

If you asked my mother to explain her religion, she would say, "I don't have the answers. I just believe."

I STARTED school at an early age. A new Catholic primary school, St. Michael's, Daceyville, was built in our area and the parish priest at the time went around the community to collect children for the new school. He came to us and my mother said, "You can take Jean because she turned 5 in November but leave Helen till next year because she has just turned 4 in December."

"Oh, no!" he said. "Mrs. Warman, you couldn't separate them. What would they do? It would break their hearts. They've been together all their lives." So, of course, what the priest or the Sisters said was what you did. I started school when I was just 4 years old. My mother took us the first few weeks and I cried all the way.

One day I said, "Mum, I'm sick. I can't go to school."

My mother said, "Okay, we'll drop Jean off and tell Sister Hyacinth." She told Sister Hyacinth that I couldn't stay because I said I was sick. Sister Hyacinth said, "Oh, poor one. Let me see." She held me and said, "Run Mrs. Warman run!" Mrs. Warman ran. I yelled and Sister Hyacinth took me in and sat me on top of a black rocking horse that was on a stand. I couldn't get down by myself. I sat there crying until Sister Hyacinth returned to give me a lolly. I was fine for the rest of the day. I hated that first year but after that I loved every minute of school.

I went to Our Lady of the Sacred Heart College Kensington for my secondary education. The teachers belonged to the same congregation as those at the primary school. I could leave after third year (intermediate) and go into nursing or become a librarian but I really wanted to be a teacher so I had to complete fourth and fifth years. I was worried about the financial pressure it put on my parents to continue at the college as there were fees to pay. My parents talked to the nuns who agreed to half fees and my textbooks would be second hand. All I'd need to buy was the uniform. Dad agreed to that and I took my school fees in an envelope every week and gave it to the nun who handled the accounts.

I DON'T REMEMBER what year I was in but I needed a tennis racquet. The athletics coach told me that I could represent Australia in tennis. I went home and I asked if it would be possible to get a new tennis racquet and Dad said, "No way." No way could we afford to get a new tennis racquet.

I said, "That's alright. I'll play the other sports." I knew the college was costing them and they were making sacrifices. One day I was called from the playground at lunch break. Sister Teresa was talking to Dad who had a smashing blue tennis racket in his hand. Sister Teresa said, "Look what your father brought you." I was speechless. It must have cost a fortune in those days. I never became the Australian champion but I played!

Helen as a schoolgirl at OLSH

WHEN WE WERE in Year 4 a new geography book came out. I remember it cost £16. I went home and remarked, "There's a new geography book just published. It costs £16."

My father said, "No way. The nuns said all your books would be second hand."

I said, "Dad, this book can't be second hand because it's new. We're the first class to use it. Nobody's ever had it before."

He said, "Good, you'll be the first student not to have it! £16!"

I went to school the next day and I told the teacher that

I didn't think I'd be getting that geography book. I went home that afternoon and my mother told me that I could get that geography book. I don't know what they did to get the £16 but the next morning I had the £16 to pay for the geography book. Our parents were so great and so good.

When I was in fifth year I approached my father to tell him I wanted to become a nun. Well, that was the end of all creation. My father wasn't a born Catholic and he immediately said, "Definitely not! You said you wanted to go to the college to become a teacher. You are not going to be a nun."

When I look back, I think that what he was thinking of really was grandchildren. Because of the rheumatic fever my sister had had, doctors said she would never play sports. She would never have children. If she had a child she would die, or the baby would die. If I became a nun, he would never have grandchildren. He needed to give his permission so until he did, I found a job.

I went to work in the office of Fossey's Department store. One day, a woman from personnel came and asked me to do a comptometer course. I thought about it and went to talk to the woman. "No, I don't think you should send me for a comptometer course, you'd better send someone else because I'm not going to be here very long."

She asked me, "Why aren't you going to be here very long?"

I said, "I want to become a nun."

The personnel officer called me into her office and said, "A nun! Oh don't be stupid. The world is at your feet! In time you could be in charge of Fossey's International, or Fossey's Australia. You have really got a great future ahead of you. You don't want to be a nun!"

I told her I wanted to be a nun. I was just waiting for my father to give his permission. She said she would drive me home that afternoon. She had a beautiful car and she was all dressed up with paint and powder and her hair was styled and she was wearing the perfect dress. Oh, she was really professional. I sat in the car. She drove me home. All the way she told me I could be anything – if I stayed on at Fossey's. I told her I didn't want to be anything, I just wanted to be a nun. That stopped her. Soon after I was offered a job at Civil Aviation. I mastered the telephone switchboard and typed out and delivered messages. I was really just waiting.

Then May came. The 31st of May was the day for entering the Novitiate and starting a new life. I asked my father again and the answer was still no. I kept on praying. The next date for entering was 21st November. November was coming close, so I said to Dad, "I really want to be a nun.'"

Dad said, "You can go, you can be a nun but I will never forgive you!" I thought to myself that at last he had said yes! I had kept in touch with the sisters at Our Lady of the Sacred Heart (OLSH) after leaving school. Once I had permission, I was accepted for the November 21st intake. My sister Jean had a boyfriend, Max, who had a little car. Mum, Jean, and Barbara, my best friend from school, and I, crammed into the back while Dad sat in the front with Max. Off we went to find Hartzer Park. We drove and drove and drove but we couldn't find the place. Then we saw a man and Dad said, "Let's stop."

We stopped and asked the fellow, "We are looking for a place called Hartzer Park."

He said, "I've been an estate agent in this area for 25 years and I have never known a place called Hartzer Park. If you find it, I'll eat my hat."

Dad said, "Good! Turn round, Max, and go back home.

There's no such place. We have been looking for a place that doesn't exist!"

I said to Max, "Keep driving, keep driving!" So Max kept driving. There on our left was Hartzer Park.

Dad said, "Stop the car and turn around!"

We asked why? He said, "Because I am going to tell that fellow to eat his bloody hat!"

We drove in. I entered. I went upstairs in a lovely dress and I came down all dressed in black. Dad nearly died. That was November. The first visiting day would be in February. He didn't come.

My mother told me not to worry. He didn't come because he was sick. The next visiting day in May he came. That was it. From then on, he accepted my choice. Every time he saw a nun, he would have to buy a bunch of bananas, a bag of apples, or a bag of tomatoes. The sisters used to tell me, "We'd be loaded up carrying things and when we met your father, he would give us a bag of bananas or tomatoes to carry." He would say "This is for my daughter."

In the early days when I was in Papua New Guinea, every month, my father would fill a box with 10 pounds of things that I couldn't get. He'd take it to the Post Office unsealed. They'd put it on the scales and he would keep putting things in until he got to the exact weight. Then he'd close it up and send it to me. The arrival of this parcel was a great event. We'd all sit round and open it.

The last box that came before Christmas always had a bottle labeled Snake Bite Medicine but it was actually rum for the Christmas pudding. Dad wrote to me every week from the time I entered until he died. He told me everything that was happening: the football score, the cricket score, who had been murdered. He sent the newspaper cuttings from the case of the Bogle and Chandler murder. As well as sending the paper cuttings, he told us what happened. It was like a serial! When the papers came the other nuns would say, "Sit down and read us what's happening!" They never found out who killed them or what happened.

(The police have now solved the case. The couple had gone to the Lane Cove River, which was polluted with a noxious gas, sulphur dioxide. They were overcome by the fumes and died. The reason the bodies were covered was because a walker with his dog had found them and moved them, making them look like they had been asleep!)

Dad also added a carton of cigarettes to the parcel when he could and I would give them to the brothers and priests. He was at a football match one day and chatted to the man beside him throughout the game. When the game was over, the man offered my father a ride home. He refused and explained he had to stop at the cigarette factory to pick up a carton to mail to me. He explained that I was a nun in Papua New Guinea. The cigarettes were for the mission. The man said, "I am the managing director so please tell them when you go to the company that you met me." From that time forward, Dad never paid for cigarettes.

The mail came to the outstations whenever a boat came. It could be one week, it could be three weeks or six weeks or three months. On the Trobriand Islands it was different because we had the weekly plane so the mail came and went on that. We never received mail in Lent. It was held. When Lent ended, the mail was handed out. When my father learned that he used to mark his envelopes 1, 2, 3, and so on because he still continued to write every week. My mother didn't write very often, only when something special was happening. She knew that my father gave me all the news. When I was at Budoya in 1972 he had a stroke and couldn't write so he dictated letters to my mother and she wrote them for him and posted them until he could do them himself again. I still have his last letter which I can hardly read.

Before I went to the missions, I didn't go home to stay. I could go and visit my family during the day but always had to return to the convent in the evening. When I returned for holidays from Papua New Guinea, I usually stayed with my family and periodically went to the convent to visit. When I went into my bedroom at home, underneath my bed would be boxes and boxes of soft drinks. Dad would have put bottles of ginger beer and lemonade under the bed. Every time he went out, he brought back bananas. I'd say to him, "Why are you bringing back bananas all the time?"

He'd say, "Oh love, I know you have bananas up in Papua New Guinea so I thought you might want them down here."

I replied, "No, I'm happy to do without them. I'd rather have apples and oranges."

My mother used to have her own bank account as well as two others. One would be called the Christmas account and the other was the Holiday account. The Christmas account went to my sister to help pay for the expenses of the Christmas meal because we always had it at her house. Every time I came home the Holiday account was there for me.

My father was very proud of me being a nun. I sent him a card for his birthday once that said '*I'm the Daddy of a Nun*' and he kept it in his wallet until he died. It was like his identity card.

I loved them and they loved me tremendously.

· · ·

I AM VERY close to my sister Jean. By the time she got to Grade 6 the sister in charge of the school suggested that she take a secretarial course including typing and shorthand. Jean went there. Mother Julianne gave the girls a great appreciation of who they were as women. She was ahead of her time and taught the girls that women were important and had a place in society and should take a stand.

Despite her health issues my sister decided that she would live a full life. She grew up very outspoken, much like Dad. She decided that if she was going to die, she would die on the playing field and not in the chair. She became a successful player on both volleyball and netball teams.

On June 8, 1956 Jean and Ted were married.

Jean had eight pregnancies. Each time she gave birth, she had all the heart specialists in Sydney around her. The first children, Gary, Jennifer, and Peter were all fine but then there was a miscarriage. After Peter, came Caroline and David, the twins. When she was pregnant Nana, Mum's mother kept saying to her, "You're carrying 2 babies."

Jean would go to the doctor and tell him what Nana had said. The doctor said it was just an old wives' tale. That went on right up until she saw the doctor on the Friday before she gave birth and he still said it was one baby. On the Sunday the twins were born. The boy was rh-negative which Jean was. This hadn't affected her other babies. They had to work quickly to give David several complete transfusions. After he was transfused the 3rd time, he died.

Twenty-one years later, my sister was in hospital with dreadful psoriasis. She looked like a skinned rabbit. I was on a 30 day retreat and asked if I could go and visit her. They gave me permission so I went. The first thing she asked me was if I had called Caroline to wish her a happy 21st birthday. I said, "Yes, as soon as I got up. I rang her and said Happy Birthday." I asked if she had. She said she had asked the nurse to make sure to wake her up early in the morning because she had to ring Caroline before she went to work. When the nurse woke Jean she asked her for the time. The nurse said, "It's 6:23." Jean said she began to cry.

When I asked her why she said, "That's the time David was born." I asked her who David was. I never met David. I'd never seen David. He had died when he was a few days old. She sat up in the bed in all this dreadful rabbit skin body and said to me, "David is my son!"

I've never forgotten it. It made a tremendous impression on me. It was 21 years after the birth of a baby that she'd hardly ever known and maybe never touched, yet she could say to me 'David is my son."

Jean and Ted and family

Gary died very suddenly in 2018. He was found dead in his apartment after a massive heart attack. Caroline died in 2019 of cancer. Jean and her husband are living in a retirement village. But she survived! She's 85!

She didn't die playing ball, and she didn't die giving birth. Every Saturday she took the kids to football or basketball or wherever they needed to go. Wherever she went, the car was always crowded with kids as there were no limits in those days. She lived a fully active life. There's always been the heart condition and the presence of what it could do but it's never done anything.

I think my father objected to me entering the Convent because he wanted those grandchildren. When Jeanie's children came along he was in raptures. He would write letters to me every week and every week he would sign with love from Mum, Dad and his royal highness (Gary), the princess (Jennifer), Prince Charming (Peter), and the ladies in waiting (Susan and Caroline). That's how he signed every letter he wrote. He loved them and would help Jean out in many ways. My sister told me she never bought a pair of school shoes for her children.

One day there was a knock on her front door. When she went out there was a man there with a refrigerator. Jean said, "I'm sorry, I haven't ordered a refrigerator. I don't have the money for one."

He said, "Is this your address?" When she said yes, he asked her if she was Mrs Large and she said she was.

"Well," said the delivery man, "That's what's on the paper so you better take it." So she took it. Dad had bought them a new refrigerator. Dad loved his five grandchildren.

Jean bought Dad great joy. They were so alike. Mum and I would be in the back of the car, Jean would be driving and Dad would be giving the instructions. He'd say, "Turn right." Jean would say, "No, it's the next turn." Dad would insist that she should turn right now. She refused. He would say, "Stop. I'll get out and walk then." Of course, he never did.

Jean has had terrible psoriasis for years but the worse she ever had it was when her eldest daughter Jennie was getting married. I went with Jean to buy a pair of shoes. At one shop, we were looking for dressy flip flops. A saleswoman came and asked if she could help.

Jean said, "I'm looking for a pair of shoes for my daughter's wedding."

The woman looked at the shoes she was trying on and said, "You can't possibly wear those to your daughter's wedding." Then my sister showed the saleswoman her feet. I've never known anyone to be so helpful. She brought out shoe after shoe for Jean to try on. Eventually, we had success. Jean dyed a turban in the kitchen sink to match the colour of her dress as she had lost all her hair to psoriasis. Her face and hands were the only parts of her body unaffected by psoriasis. She wore a dress with a high neck and long sleeves as well as gloves. My Auntie Bet watched my sister going from table to table visiting with the wedding guests. She asked me, "Is she really as bad as they say she is?"

"Yes, Auntie Bet," I said, "She really is as bad as they say. She's covered in it."

That was the worst time she ever had. But it flared up when Gary and Carolyn died. Her back is bad and sometimes when I go home, she asks me to rub ointment on it. It's hard even to look at. I don't think it is painful but the itch is so bad you just want to tear your back out. She never complained about it. It has never stopped her from doing anything with her husband, her children or her family.

. . .

I SPENT 2000 in Australia with Mum who had turned 90. I thought it was time to give her some of my time, so I came home. When Dad died in February 1987, the parish priest said to me, "You know, your father has gone now. Your mother's by herself and you've spent so many years in Papua New Guinea, it's time for you to come back and spend time with your mother."

I thought about it. I went home, and said to Mum, "Mum, would you like me to come back and spend time in Australia and be close to you?"

Her answer was, "Your father would never ask you to do that."

Yet, my father had been the one who had been against me going to Papua New Guinea but now she was saying that your father would never ask you to leave and come home to be with us. They knew what Papua New Guinea meant to me.

I didn't come down right away but in 2000, when she turned 90 and conveniently the Olympic Games were on in Australia, in Sydney, I came and stayed for a year with my mother.

She sold the old house and had this lovely little villa, close to the beach and close to shopping areas, and lovely for early morning walks. I stayed there with her and I went back to our convent in Kensington for a weekend every month. We had a great year, Mum, Jean and I.

When I was growing up, we did everything together. My parents would say to us we would do this or that on the weekend. My father always took his holidays during the school holidays so we could go away together. We did everything as a family. We sat around the table and had a meal as a family. But now people sit around the television or look at their phones or Ipads while they eat. I think families have lost the closeness that I was lucky to have.

---

1. 1 *__Rhesus Factor__ In 1937 the Rhesus factor (a protein on red blood cells) was discovered. It was noticed that a Rhesus negative mother (who does not have the protein on her red blood cells) with a Rhesus positive partner may have one or two normal pregnancies but then becomes unable to carry another baby to term. Some of the baby's Rhesus positive red blood cells cross over from the placenta near the time of delivery and the mother develops antibodies to the protein. This does not usually affect the first or second pregnancy, but subsequent pregnancies increase the antibody response and these antibodies cross over the placenta and destroy the baby's red blood cells leading to severe anemia, multiple organ failure, and premature death. Rhesus immune globulin was developed in the 1960's and is now routinely given to Rhesus negative women during pregnancy, significantly reducing the infant mortality.

TWO
POSTULANT
HARTZER PARK, AUSTRALIA NOVEMBER 1953 - MAY 1959

I KNEW from the very beginning that I wanted to be a Sister in the congregation of The Daughters of Our Lady of the Sacred Heart (OLSH). The congregation had been founded by Father Jules Chevallier in Issoudun, France in 1874. Under the direction of Mother Superior Marie Louise Hartzer, the Sisters arrived in Australia in 1885. I had been taught by wonderful teachers at St Michael's Primary and OLSH College and they were all Sisters. I admired them greatly.

I entered the convent at Hartzer Park on November 21, 1953. We spent six months as Postulants, which meant we were just looking and getting an idea of what religious life would be like. At the end of six months we then became Novices which would last for 12 months.

I was a Novice from July 1954 to July 1955. We studied what religious life meant as well as theology, the Bible and the story of the congregation we were entering. There were 10 in our group and that was considered quite big. There was an entry every six months so there were always three groups: the Postulants, 1st year Novices and

2nd year Novices, the ones getting ready to make their vows. We did some studies together and some separately as Postulants. I didn't find it particularly difficult.

Sister Helen as a Postulant

I look back now and I know that it was what I always really wanted. Visiting days were every three months. We thought that was marvellous. It was harder on our parents than it was on us because we were where we wanted to be, whereas they were losing what they had.

My parents came up religiously every three months. I remember one time my young cousin came up with his mother, Auntie Sheila, who was Mum's youngest sister. He didn't say much the whole time he was there. He just stood behind his mother and every now and again he would punctuate his silence with, "But Mum, hasn't she got fat."

By the end of the afternoon he had me convinced that I'd really put on weight. I don't know why because we went from dawn to dusk. We had a marvelous time but we were on the go all the time, cleaning the house, working in the gardens and orchards, in the dairy, looking after the chickens and collecting firewood, studying and doing written assignments. It was a great time.

ON THE 2ND JULY, 1955, I made my first vows and left the Novitiate. I moved to Kensington, in Sydney, the Mother House of the OLSH Australian Province. Our OLSH congregation had primary and secondary schools across Australia. The Catholic Education Sector at that time was controlled by the Catholic Church. We followed the government curriculum because the students had to write government exams but the church could just put teachers in and take them out. Each congregation controlled its own schools.

When I arrived in Kensington, a Sister teaching in a nearby school was sent to the missions, so I was told I was going to teach on Monday. Over the weekend I had some quick lessons and on Monday I went to the school with another sister. Julie and I were in the same group. For a week we watched and at the beginning of the next week we started giving lessons. She had Preps (Kindergarten) and I had Grade 1. Unfortunately for her she had no control in the classroom. I don't know what it was but when I walked into a classroom I had total control. After a week or so, we changed classes – Julie took Grade 1 and I took preps.

One morning one of my small students was lying on the floor screaming in an effort to get his mother to take him back home. His anxious mother was standing over him. I kept repeating, "Go Mrs Smith. Go! I'll look after him. He'll be right as soon as you go."

Just then my old Prep teacher, now in charge of this Infants School, walked by and said, with a twinkle in her eye, "I'll not lift a finger to help you. This is what you did to me so often in your early days." When the mother had gone, the screaming ceased. I reached down a hand and helped a small boy to his feet. As I dried the tears before joining the class I looked up and received an encouraging nod from my wonderful mentor.

Another time, we were at an assembly and nobody was moving. I didn't realize that my class was supposed to move first. I was just standing there and suddenly Sister Hyacinth, who was standing at the front and leading the assembly, called out "Helen Warman move your class!" Everybody looked around to find out who this person was. Nobody knew who Helen Warman was. You never knew Sisters' original names, you just knew them by their religious names. I'd taken the name Dorothy when I became a sister and so I was Sister Dorothy not Sister Helen. So, I moved my class and I became Sister Dorothy again. I stayed at that school for just 12 months and then went to Melbourne.

Melbourne had a very special system that they called JT – Junior Teachers. Instead of going to teacher's college, you went straight into the classroom. Every week you were given a demonstration lesson by one of the teachers on staff and every week you gave a lesson. The person supervising you came in to watch your lesson and wrote up a critique. Upon completion of each year a government inspector would come to observe you teaching a lesson.

At the end of the second year, there was a written exam on a book by Elijah and Cole. I walked around with this great thick volume under my arms for two years. It's a wonder I'm not deformed from carrying it around. If you passed then you became a registered teacher.

The Victorian JT Teaching Certificate was recognized worldwide. It really was a good way of learning how to teach because you were actually doing it all the time. Some of our sisters trained in Melbourne. Other sisters stayed at Kensington and attended a small private teacher's college nearby. They had psychology and art lessons. We missed out on those, but in the long run, I think JTs turned out better classroom teachers. We might not have had the finer points in some things but I know I never regretted that I did that kind of training. From the very beginning, we were dealing with parents and children in the classroom. I think that's when my love of children in the classroom began. I stayed there at St. Edmond's, Croydon in Melbourne for two and a half years until the end of 1958. I returned to the Novitiate at Hartzer Park to take my final vows in July 1958.

I remember Mum saying to me, "Are you going to wear a bridal gown because I've still got my wedding frock?" Our ceremony was quite simple and we didn't dress as brides. My parents and Jean and her family came and I remember walking along the verandah of the room that was set up for the reception after the ceremony. Every Sister who made their final vows had a cake on the table. I saw this beautiful cake on the table with a light shining inside it. I thought "Oh, if only I could have a cake like that." When I went inside I found out that it was my cake. My uncle's friend decorated cakes and he had decorated it for me.

WHEN I WAS in the Novitiate, the Novice Mistress, a lovely woman, said to me "Do you want to go to the

Missions?" I replied, "No, I don't want to go to the Missions, I want to stay in Australia."

You had to ask to go to the Missions. You weren't just sent. I remember saying to her, "I have changed my mind. I think I'd really like to go to the Missions." After final vows, I returned to Croydon for six months. I could have been sent to Kiribati, Papua New Guinea, or the Northern Territory in Australia. You weren't given a choice of where you went. They were the three big Australian Missions at the time.

During that time, I was told that at the end of the year, I would be going to Papua New Guinea. I was very blessed because I went to Eastern Papua, and to me, that was the jewel in the crown.

They were extraordinary times, really. You didn't question. That's why you entered. You made a vow of poverty, chastity and obedience so if you were told to go to Papua New Guinea that is where you went.

At the end of the year I returned to Kensington, where during a large ceremony, a large group of us received our mission cross. Three were going to Manus Island in northern Papua New Guinea, several were going to other parts of Papua New Guinea and the others were going to the Northern Territory.

This was the first time Manus had opened up since the Second World War. Three Dutch Sisters had been on Manus during the war and they had been picked up by a Japanese boat, the *Akikaze*, to be taken to the concentration camp on Rabaul Island, Papua New Guinea in March 1943. The boat also picked up a number of Lutheran missionaries along the north coast of Manus Island. Neither the Sisters nor the Lutheran missionaries were ever heard of again.

After the war the captain of the boat said that he was

told that he was not to have passengers on board when he arrived in Rabaul. So 51 missionaries were all shot and dropped overboard between Kavieng and Rabaul. Some of the sailors on the boat were Buddhists and they had joined the navy because they felt that it was the least combative force. When they got to Rabaul they held a Buddhist ceremony to cleanse the boat because of the lives that had been lost. For years no one knew what had happened to them but the story came out when the war trials were held.

In 1959 when we went to the mission we would stay for 10 years before we could come back to Australia. Sister Boniface said to my mother and father, "Don't worry. I remember in the old days when we stood on this verandah and cried as we said goodbye because we knew that we would never see our family again." My father said, "Small consolation." The times were changing. My first trip back to Australia was after 5 years in Papua New Guinea. After that, I returned almost every two years.

I was excited to get to my first posting, I learned it was a mission school in a place called Daio in Milne Bay Province.

THREE
DAIO, MILNE BAY PROVINCE
JANUARY 1959 - JUNE 1963

I REMEMBER LEAVING Sydney at 9 o'clock at night on a DC3. We landed at Brisbane and picked up two of our Sisters who were also returning to Milne Bay. Apparently, we had a frightful electrical storm.

The plane flew in the air like a piece of paper. It flew this way and that way and there was thunder and lightning and I slept through the lot. Sister Patricia Clark who was sitting beside me said the hostess kept coming back to see if I was all right. She eventually asked Sister Patricia if she should wake me up. Sister Patricia said, "No, then she'll be scared." I slept through the whole lot. That was my first plane flight.

We arrived at Jackson's Airport in Port Moresby, where there was just a tier of seats where people could sit. There were so many people travelling to Milne Bay that they had two planes. One plane flew directly to Samarai, a Catalina that landed directly on the sea. The second plane flew directly to Gurney – the airstrip for Alotau. Then the Catalina that had landed in Samarai flew to Gurney and picked up the passengers and flew us to Samarai. We landed on the water just by the wharf. The Catalina was a wonderful plane. It could land either on water or land.

When I got to Samarai I was taken to the Sisters' house. I was finally able to open my suitcase and change from my black habit to the much lighter white one. We then left for Sideia, the main mission station, about 1 ½ hours away. From Sideia, the mission boat would take me to Daio, about 3 hours by boat from either Samarai or Sideia. If you look on the map, Daio is exactly opposite Alotau.

Samarai was called the 'Pearl of the Pacific' and you could walk around it in about 10 minutes. It had beautiful frangipani trees and a couple of hills. The hospital was on top of one hill and the dentist was at the bottom. Samarai had two stores, one was Steamships and the other was called BPs (Burns Phillip). It would take you all day to do your shopping because you'd go to one and find out the price and then go to the other and find the price. Then, you'd have to decide where you were going to buy each thing.

There was a convent in Daio where I lived. It was right on the water, a beautiful place. Daio had a stone beach and I remember thinking that I would never sleep because when the tide came in and went out and passed over the stones there was noise as the stones moved with the water. But after a while I slept and never even noticed it.

I TAUGHT Grade 1 at Sacred Heart Primary School and shared a wall with Aloysius, the Prep or Kindergarten teacher.

It took me ages to figure things out. I would say 'Sit down' to the students, and they would all say 'Sit down' and nobody would move. I would move my hands and say 'Sit down' and they would all move their hands and say "Sit down"and no one would sit down. Finally, I sat down and I said, "Sit down" and the students sat down and all of them said "Sit down." "Yes," I said, "That's right. Sit down."

The first year I was there I had the little ones but later on I taught grades 3 and 4. But the little ones were so beautiful, so accepting. They were lovely to teach. Years later, I was at Hagita and nurses came out from Alotau to collect blood donations. I was walking down the road and met this nurse's aide who was there helping them. She had been one of the girls I taught in Grade 1. She asked me where I was going and I said that I was going to give blood. She said, "Oh, my grandmother. You are too old to give blood but you come and sit beside the students that give blood to give them comfort and support but you cannot give blood. You are too old." I suppose I was about 60 then but I was young and beautiful when I first went to teach Grade 1 and now she was a married woman with children and I looked like a grandmother.

MY STUDENTS DIDN'T HAVE much English but it was such fun teaching them. One time there was a visiting priest from Germany who watched one of my lessons. It was a religion lesson on the Ascension of Jesus. I took the children down to the sea and explained that Jesus got up and He walked and walked and when He got to the bottom of the hill He went up to Heaven. I went on with all this lovely talk and we all marched around the place and had a lovely time. When we had finished the visiting priest said to me, "You're just wasting your time they don't understand a word you're saying. We should be speaking in their language."

I didn't know enough of the language to really give a lesson so the next day, I asked one of the priests who was fluent in the local language to take my class and find out what they know about Ascension. The next day he took the class out under a tree and they rolled on the grass and they laughed and they had a marvellous time and he talked and talked and they talked and talked and they laughed. At the end he said, "They know everything that you've said."

I think you can talk and talk and get across to people what you're saying even though it's not in their language as long as they've got a little bit of the language and you use a lot of acting. We had work parade every day for one hour. The children were given jobs to do around the school. As we didn't have much to do, the children would teach me their language and I would teach them the English words. Often, we'd roll on the ground laughing at what I was saying in their language.

Aloysius and I had a classroom which had a half way wall between us. He had a very bad leg with elephantiasis. Elephantiasis is caused by the filarial worm which is transmitted from human to human by the female mosquito. It causes swelling in the arms and legs.

Aloysius used to carry this great big heavy leg around with him. He was a wonderful, wonderful man. Everybody used to say that you could always tell children who had been taught by him because they knew their times tables. I would hear him chant with the children: It would be 2 1s are two, 2 2s are 4, all the way through to 12 1s are 12, 12 2s are 24, 12 12s are 144. If the children started again, I would know he had fallen asleep. Then off they'd start again.

THERE WERE two big things that happened when I was

at Daio. One happened the first year I was there. On the 5th September 1959, Sister Verona died of black water fever.

Black water fever is a complication of malaria. The person's urine is black or dark red which is caused by the large amounts of hemoglobin released when the person's red blood cells are destroyed by malarial parasites.

That was my first introduction to death. Mum's father and Dad's mother had died but they were the only two in my family and I hadn't really been connected with either of the deaths. I loved both of them especially Nana, Dad's mother. She was a beautiful woman but she died up at Mittagong and I was in Sydney and very young and I really didn't know what death was. When my grandfather died, my sister and I and a couple of older cousins stayed at home and minded the younger ones and had a party in the backyard.

Sister Verona was the one in charge of our convent in Daio. Sister Verona had started up a women's club. It met on Wednesday afternoons. When she arrived back at the convent after the meeting one day, Sister Bernadine, who worked in the hospital, took one look at her and said, "You look awful. Go to bed."

Sister Verona had tea and went off to bed. The next morning she got up and came down to breakfast and she was yellow. Her eyes were as yellow as I don't know what. Sister Bernadine told her she couldn't go to school and to go back to bed. On Friday, Sister Bernadine told her she had blackwater fever because she had seen blood in her urine. Sister Verona said, "I can't have blackwater fever. I had it when I first came up at Ladava and I had to stay in bed for two weeks. How can I stay in bed for two weeks here?" That's what she said, I heard her.

Now when I said that later, nobody who'd been with

her in those early days could ever remember her having blackwater fever. They say if you have blackwater once, you must leave the country. You don't wait to get it twice because if you get it again, it's fatal. By Friday night she was really bad. She had a raging fever. Sister Bernadine went to see Father to ask him to send the mission boat up to Samarai to get medical help as Daio didn't have any radio contact. He agreed and the boat planned on leaving at 4 am the next morning. We waited up but didn't hear the boat leave at 4 am. At about 6 am we heard the boat go past. There had been some mechanical problem. The boat was going to Sideia and when it got there, Sideia was able to contact Samarai and tell them that there was a Sister at Daio with blackwater fever and ask for medical assistance. They said they would send a doctor right away in the government boat which was much faster than the mission boat.

At 3 o'clock Sister Bernadine asked our priest to come and give Sister Verona the Last Rites. He came and he anointed her. To me, that's when Sister Verona died. I remember that her eyes changed completely. It was as if someone pulled a blind down over them. At about 5 o'clock, the boat arrived. I remember it being really rough that day and the government boat couldn't come in and it anchored offshore. The medical team got into the dingy and in my memory, the village men had to swim out, get a hold of the dingy and pull it into shore.

The doctor wanted to do a blood transfusion but no one knew their blood type except a priest who said he was 'O' type – the universal donor. He gave blood and they went to give it to Sister Verona and the blood spilt all over the floor. When they tried to put it in, all her veins had collapsed. At 6 o'clock she officially died. But I always say, she died at 3 o'clock because her whole faced changed, her whole body just collapsed. I'd never seen anyone die before. Even though her heart was still beating until 6 o'clock, to me, she died at 3 o'clock.

At one point, Sister Bernadine wondered if Sister Verona should be moved to the hospital at Samarai. She had me look it up in a textbook. It said that if you moved someone with blackwater fever, you might as well build a tombstone. You can't move anyone with blackwater fever. They have to stay where they are. The next morning at about 6 o'clock the local men came to collect the body and they took it down to Wagga Wagga which was the next government station, going east towards Gurney. She could be loaded on the boat easily there. We walked in the opposite direction and the boat picked us up at Giligili. From there, we went to Sideia where she was buried.

THE SECOND BIG thing that happened at Daio was quite different. In 1962, a Sister came to Daio who had been teaching in Port Moresby for many years. Her school was right in Port Moresby and she could walk down the hill and be at the big international wharf quite quickly. Every time a big ship came into the wharf, she took her children down to see these ships. Sometimes, they were able to go on board. They had a marvelous time. And then she came to Daio.

She was teaching her Grade 5 students one day, and she asked them if they had ever seen a big ship. They said, "Oh, yes, Sister." And she asked them, "What's the biggest ship you've ever seen?" And the students said, "*Morning Star*." *Morning Star* was the cargo ship for the mission. It had a cabin with a couple of bunks and it had room for cargo in its hold.

To the students, the *Morning Star* was big. So she came home from school and said, "I am going to write to the Admiral of the Fleet in Australia, and tell him that this is Milne Bay where the Australian forces fought during the war and please, could some Australian ship come up to Milne Bay." She wrote the letter and sent it on the boat to Samarai. A few weeks later, the mission boat arrived with cargo and mail and there was a letter from the Admiralty that the HMAS *Voyageur* would be returning to Australia from Japan where it had been doing exercises and it would be calling into Milne Bay. The children from the school would be invited on board.

It came round East Cape early, early in the morning when it was still dark. It was all lit up like a blazing city, a floating city coming down Milne Bay. We were all sitting out on the beach at 4 o'clock in the morning watching this magnificent ship sail down the bay. At 6:30 Father Murphy came by and asked if anyone was coming for Mass. I said, "Yes, the sisters and I will come for Mass but the children will stay." We went over and had Mass and then went for breakfast. The children had breakfast quickly and then flew back to the beach.

The HMAS *Voyageur* was a huge ship and the sister ship of the HMAS *Melbourne*, the aircraft carrier. The children were all dressed up in their best uniforms. The girls were in green skirts and the boys wore green trousers. No one wore tops. The barges from the ship came to the beach and the children got on and went out to the ship. They climbed up the side and they got on board. We came out in the mission boat, the *Stella Maris*, and climbed up. Then the children looked over the side of the ship and they could see the tiny little matchbox way down in the sea and they asked me what it was. I told them it was the Stella *Maris*. They said, "No, too small, too small." We were so high up.

Our day began. We flew up Milne Bay in that big ship. We got to Samarai in an hour. If we'd gone on one of our boats it would have taken four hours. They let off torpedoes from the back of the boat. They sent flares into the sky. The boys played the ack-ack guns. We had a marvelous time. We had afternoon tea with cakes and soft drinks. The officers showed us the boat. One of the officers came and said, "Sisters, I'm very sorry but we have a problem."

I said, "What's the problem?"

He said, "Well, we have a souvenir for the students."

I said, "That's really good. What is it?"

He said, "It's a tie pin and they have no tops."

I said, "That's all right. They can put in on the bands of their skirts or the bands of their trousers."

"Oh, good," he said. So they all got their souvenir.

Now, Jacqueline was a student there at the school in Grade 5. Many years later she was a teacher in the Trobriand Islands. I came out from Mass one morning and Jacqueline came running up to me and said, "Sister, they've killed our ship. They've killed our ship."

What had happened was the Australian navy had been having exercises in Melbourne. There had been a dreadful mix up with orders and the *HMAS Melbourne* had gone across and somehow cut the *HMAS Voyageur* in half. Many sailors on the *HMAS Voyageur* were killed. It was a real tragedy.

Seeing the *HMAS Voyageur* was one of the highpoints of our lives. Jacqueline never forgot her ship.

Three and a half years later, my time at Daio came to an end. I was sent to Budoya on Fergusson Island.

FOUR

BUDOYA, MILNE BAY PROVINCE

JUNE 1963 - DECEMBER 1964; JANUARY 1972 - DECEMBER 1972

I FIRST ARRIVED at the Catholic Mission at Budoya on Fergusson Island in June 1963 to teach at Our Lady of the Sacred Heart School.

Soon after I arrived at Budoya, I met Maria Agatha Franziska Gobertina von Trapp. She was the second oldest daughter of Captain von Trapp, and was called Lisel in *The Sound of Music*. *The Sound of Music* is a famous musical that tells the story of the Von Trapp family and their journey to freedom in World War Two. In real life, the Von Trapp family later went on tour as singers. At the conclusion of the Von Trapp Family Singers' Australian tour, the family met one of the Milne Bay priests. Maria and her two half siblings decided to become mission workers.

Maria was living in a bush material house at Budoya. Her half-brother, Johannes, was a carpenter who helped with building until he returned to the United States for military service. Rosemarie, her half- sister, helped out at the school until she left because of the isolation. Maria stayed for 14 years and taught singing to the students and interested villagers.

Maria took the children for singing several times a week in school time. When I arrived she invited me to come to her class. I went to watch. She put these numbers on the board - 1, 4, 6, 7, 3, 2, 15. Then she said to the children, "Now sing" and they did. I was flabbergasted because there was nothing except numbers on the board and here they were, singing this tune. I asked her how they could sing like that. She introduced me to the Tonic Sol-Fa system and explained that the numbers were the notes. This was how Maria (the nun) taught the Von Trapp children in the *Sound of Music* to sing – *doe, a deer a female deer, ray, a drop of golden sun, me, a name I call myself ...* This was it. That was all she ever did to teach the children a song.

There was a singing competition at Es'ala, the government station on Fergusson. Maria taught them a new song by putting the numbers on the blackboard and the children sang the tune, then she added the words under the numbers. They sang, "The Little Drummer Boy." If I taught them a song, I would have to sing it over and over. The children would have to sing it after me. I never learned her system but greatly admired it.

AT BUDOYA, there were few ways of generating school funds. We heard from another school of their success with growing chillies. We decided to grow our own. The boys and I spent an afternoon clearing a garden and then planting chilies. When I got out of bed the next morning, I knew something wrong. My feet didn't feel right. I tried to look at my feet but my eyes wouldn't open properly. I called for Sister Ben (Benedicta) to come. My feet were huge, my eyes were swollen shut and my mouth was all swollen as were my lips.

Sister Ben told me to go back to bed. She went to the boys' dormitory to tell them I wouldn't be coming. She found the boys sitting on their mats with these great big pudgy hands in front of them. They thought the spirits were in them. Sister Ben told them I was exactly the same. She said, "Go back to bed. It's only from the chilies." We never got much out of the chillies because everybody was terrified to touch them.

One day we were out working, doing something in the school grounds, cleaning up or cutting grass. I had brown stockings on. The girls were whispering all around me. Eventually, one of them came up and rubbed my leg. She turned round to the others and she said, "Not true, not true. Not like ours." I had brown legs like theirs' but it wasn't skin. It was the stockings.

ANOTHER TIME I was teaching a lesson and the children interrupted me and said, "Look out the window."

I said, "We're learning, not looking out the window." They insisted so I looked out. There was one of those little tornadoes, just a small one, spinning up the path.

At that same moment , one of the nurses started to burn the rubbish from the hospital. The little tornado picked up the fire and went up the hill, setting it ablaze. Then it swept to the east, burning everything in its path. It went for miles and then changed direction. We received a message saying that it was coming back our way.

The men made a fire break between the school and the village. The boys climbed on the sago leaf roofs and drenched them with water. The fire came back and jumped the fire break and set the buildings on fire. We ran up and down most of the night with buckets of water, filling them up at the pump and then throwing the water on the fire. Sister Ben who was very tall ran in front and I was running behind. I suddenly dropped into a hole. It was a drain, a great big one. Sister Benedicta shouted "Where are you, Helen?"

"I'm here," I shouted, "in a big hole." She had jumped over it with her big long legs but mine were too short to make it across so I went down. As the fire burned, wild pigs came out of the bush and into the school grounds. The boys had a fantastic time chasing these wild pigs and catching a few. That night we had wild pig for tea.

The whole of Fergusson Island is a mass of extinct volcanoes. It had beautiful hot springs where we would go just to see them. On the way, I remember that there were lots of carnivorous plants, lots and lots of pitcher plants that insects fell into.

When tourists go, they should have guides to make sure they stay on solid ground. There are very thin crusts of crystalline sulphur. Your foot would be seriously burnt if it went into hot sulphur. At times we would go there for a picnic, wrap our yams (or whatever we had to cook) in leaves and put them into the springs. While we waited for our food to cook we would swim in the beautiful warm water of the river. I don't know what else was in the water. It could have killed us, I suppose, with all the minerals from the hot springs but we never thought about it. We would come back and pull our food out of the hot springs and eat it. It was delicious. Despite what was in the water, sulphur I suppose, I am still alive to tell the tale.

Several times at Budoya, we were put on alert to move because of volcanic activity. Once, there were Australian naval ships in the area standing by in case there was an eruption. There were volcanoes on land directly behind the mission station at Budoya and opposite us at Salamo. The one that caused the alerts was in the sea between Budowya and Salamo. It never erupted but we did get some terrible shakes. The refrigerator really danced in the kitchen at Budoya.

I had been at Budoya for 2 years when word came in April 1965 that I was to go to the Trobriand Islands to teach at St. Anthony's School at Gusaweta.

FIVE
THE TROBRIAND ISLANDS, MILNE BAY PROVINCE

JANUARY 1965 - DECEMBER 1971; JANUARY 1980 - FEBRUARY 1984

SISTER MARGUERITE CAME and told me that I was going to the Trobriand Islands on the Friday before Palm Sunday. I would be teaching Grade 4. I was replacing Sister Peter Mary. She wasn't happy going and I wasn't happy coming.

There are four main islands in the group and a number of small ones. Collectively, everybody just calls them the Trobs.

The mission boat, the *Morning Star,* dropped me at the Losuia wharf on Kiriwina Island on a Saturday. An old army jeep drove me to the mission station at Gusaweta. Everyone came running over. I got out and walked towards the convent.

I can remember this tiny tot who had been left behind in the house crying, "I want to come. I want to come." Someone picked her up and brought her over. Later I found out she was Loretto. Her mother had breast cancer. Dr Junter, a wonderful German doctor, wanted to remove her breast, but her people said "No!" You can't have a woman walking around with only one breast." No! It's just wasn't going to happen.

When Loretto was born, the mother died. Before she died she asked Sister Xavier, the sister in charge, to take Loretto. She was afraid that she would end up being a 'water girl', carrying water and doing chores for another family. Sister Xavier took this little tot from the time she was just a few weeks old. Loretto stayed in the convent until she completed Grade 5 when she left for Sideia. Later on, she went to Hagita to complete high school. A few years later, she married and had 5 children. After her husband's death, she supported her family by working in an administration position.

IT DIDN'T TAKE me long to enjoy the Trobs. Everyone was curious and asked questions: who are you, how old are you, where did you come from, what's your mother's name, what's your father's name, how many children in your family? They wanted to know everything about me so it made me feel at home. They were so friendly. There was no holding back with them. I loved the place but it was the people who won my heart.

When I first arrived at the Trobs, I was very wary of the people. The mission school at St Anthony's, Gusaweta was a weekly boarding school. The inland children walked in every Sunday evening and walked home again on Friday afternoon. At the time, the mission had one old discarded army jeep. Father would drive out to the villages and collect the children's food.

The mothers of the children from nearby villages would bring a pot of food for the evening meal and food wrapped in a banana leaf for the morning. While waiting for their children to come and collect the food, the women would sit on the cement top of an underground tank near the convent and talk.

Their conversation sounded like a war to me. One day I asked Sister Xavier, "What are they fighting about?"

She replied, "They're not fighting, they're just talking".

GRADUALLY, I began to go out and talk to them. Many of the Trob women who lived close to the mission spoke English. They had most likely gone to the mission school which had been there since 1934. All of the women who worked with us could speak English.

Some of the women did the washing and ironing. One day they came across this item to iron. They went to see Sister Xavier who was in charge and asked, "Do you know what the sisters are wearing?"

Sister Xavier said, "They're wearing their habit."

The women asked whether she knew what they were wearing under their habit. Sister Xavier said, "No."

They said, "They are wearing these!" They held up this divided skirt. It was really beautifully made. One of our Sisters who was a great seamstress had made the divided skirts. They were really cool to wear. When we put them on, you couldn't tell that it wasn't a skirt. They were worn underneath our habit so it couldn't be seen in any case. The women still refused to iron them and said the sisters would have to iron them themselves.

Sister Xavier said, "Fine, they can do that but if they don't wear them, when they go out on the motorbike, their skirts will come up over their knees and everybody will see their legs."

"Oh," said the women. After that the pants were ironed.

In those days, women just didn't wear slacks, pants or even shorts. It seemed awful to them that the nuns were wearing pants, even under their habit.

ONE DAY the school inspector visited our school. He asked the students if they knew what an encyclopedia was. No one knew. Then he asked if they knew about Bronislaw Malinowski. Malinowski was an anthropologist who had stayed on the Trobs for a number of years during WWI and had written several textbooks on the lives of the Trobriand Islanders. My students didn't know that either. The inspector was pretty disgusted the students didn't know these things. After his departure, I decided to take the students over to Father's house as he had a great library of Malinowski's books. The children couldn't read them because the English was so hard. But there were pictures in the books of the old people as well as the villages. We had a great time looking at these.

About a week later we were in school and one of the boys said to me, "Sister, there's a white lady walking round the playground." I told them to keep working as I went to ask what she wanted.

I went out and asked, "Can I help you?"

She said, "I'm just having a look around. I'm Malinowski's daughter, Helena." I nearly fainted! I took her into the classroom and announced, "This is Malinowski's daughter." The children were astounded.

I said, "Now, you can ask her anything you want."

The students bombarded her with questions. She answered them all. She told them that ever since she was a little girl her father had told her stories about the Trobriand Islands. Now she had come to see if they were true. She went off and spent time in the villages. Later she came back to us. "Well," we asked, "are the stories true?"

She nodded. "Yes. I saw the mother's baby coat, the one the mother wears like a shawl for three months after giving birth. I went into the house of a mother who had just given birth and she was wearing this coat."

Woman wearing baby cape, Trobs. (Image courtesy JT Goddard)

When I first went to the Trobs, I thought the custom of the baby coat was dreadful because of the isolation it imposed on the woman and child. When a woman gave birth, she remained inside a one room house for three months. Her only company was her baby and her family members when they came to bring food. She only left the house when it was dark to use the toilet. No one could see her because it would make her family look bad, that they couldn't look after her and the baby properly.

After a while I realized what a wonderful bonding time this was between the mother and her child. For three months all the mother did was look after the child, wash the child, feed the child, hold the child. I remember listening to a doctor speak on the radio explaining that when babies are born they shouldn't be all wrapped up. There should be skin to skin contact with the mother. The baby should feel the mother's skin. The baby should be put naked on the mother's breast so it can feel the skin. That's what happens on the Trobriand Islands, skin on skin. A truly beautiful custom. After three months the mother is taken down to the sea, for a washing ceremony. She is then given a special covering made out of coconut leaves to wear. This is so that the spirits cannot see her breasts and spoil the milk.

Helena also saw the bundles of *doba* or women's wealth. The *doba* was an uncompleted skirt made out of banana leaves for the *sagali*. The doba was a described as a "Trobriand bundle of sorrow." The *doba* wasn't worn, but was passed from one *sagali* to another. A *sagali* was a feast to mark the end of the time of mourning after a family death. During the *sagali*, the *doba* was given as gifts to those who in some way shared in the family's grief.

In those days, most of the cooking was still done in clay pots. The food the people ate was much the same as her father had told her: yams. She saw the yam gardens, the yams being carried into the villages, and placed in cone shaped piles beside the yam house. She told us she could see that all those stories her father had told her were true. She went off happy and left the children feeling very proud of their way of life.

A few weeks later another fellow came. I went to the

playground to meet him. He was a professor from some university in Melbourne who was teaching about the Trobriand Islands where he had never been. He was teaching out of books so he decided to come to the Trobs and see for himself what life was like. He did the same thing. He went out to a village, stayed there, then came back and said, "Well, now, I can go back and tell my students that everything I've been teaching them is just a pack of lies."

He had exactly the opposite experience to Malinowski's daughter. She saw everything her father had told her as true and he saw everything he read in the books as false. The Trobriand people have always been very aware of people's attitudes towards them and their way of life. It would seem that Helena was totally open to all they shared with her, but the professor was just a closed book, so saw and learnt nothing.

IN 1969, when my parents came to the Trobs I was so excited. I wanted to take them to watch the big ocean-going Kula canoes leave on their trading voyage. I remembered from previous years, when the men went away for Kula, the women had a marvelous time. They would go from village to village and take food and come back with food. They would visit and make doba as they talked. Although everyone wept as the men left, it was a real relief for the women when the men weren't around.

We missed seeing the canoes leave there because the blessed truck broke down. The driver of a car that came along said he had room for one person in the car. We decided that Dad would go to the mission for help. Mum and I would wait with the truck. We waited on the veranda of an old trade store that had been closed down. People brought us bananas to eat and coconut juice to drink. They came and sat with us and looked after us.

Mum said, "What are they sitting here for?"

I explained, "They're looking after us. They're making sure we're ok." We talked a bit. I told them who she was and they shook hands. It was ages before help came. When Fr Murphy did arrive, he said, "I'm sure if I sit in that truck and turn the key it will start." But that didn't happen and he ended up towing us back to the mission.

We had another trip out when Mum insisted on sitting in the back of the truck rather than in the cab. I told her it would be rough for someone who was 59 at that time. A couple of days later she asked me to have a look at her back as it felt a bit sore. She was black and blue from her neck to her waist from being on the back of that truck!

My parents stayed in a guest cabin close to the mission and had meals at the convent. Our electricity came from a generator and every night it would be shut off. They had a torch to help them to find their way to the cabin. After a few days my mother said that they weren't sleeping well. I thought perhaps the noises from the insects and frogs were bothering them. It turned out that it was the complete darkness that happened once the lights went out. It was worse if there was no moon. We found a little hurricane lamp and as long as it was burning they could sleep.

Brother McCann, one of the Catholic Brothers who worked at the mission station, invited us to watch a cricket match. Dad said, "Oh, no. I can see cricket any day of the week when I am home."

I said to him, "You haven't seen cricket played like this before." I explained, "It's different here. The players wear their traditional clothes. Instead of having 11 players on each side, they have 60 or 70. The ball is a smooth, round piece of wood, unlike the Australian cricket ball which is made of cork with a layer of tightly woven string covered by a leather case. The bat is like a softball bat, carved out of a piece of wood from the bush. There are two wickets, one at each end of the field. At the end of the game and every time a six was hit, the winning team performs a victory dance. The batsman tries to hit the ball, and if he succeeds, he runs between the two wickets, scoring points. The score is kept by cutting off fronds from a coconut palm leaf. The home team has to win. The visitors have to lose in a way that shows they really would have won if they weren't being polite."

After that description, Dad decided that he'd come for the drive.

When we arrived, a great crowd had gathered. Each team had their socks painted on and were all traditionally dressed. There were people of every age and size playing on each team. There were fellows on the side keeping score by cutting off the fronds from the coconut palm leaf. Brother McCann stood there a while and then he said, "I'm going home. Are you coming Ern?"

My father said, " No. I'll stay with Helen for a while and see what happens."

Trob cricket. (Image courtesy of JT Goddard.)

We had a marvelous time watching Trobriand Island cricket. Dad enjoyed watching them use a wooden bat and ball, people getting hit and falling to the ground. At lunchtime Brother McCann returned to take us home for lunch.

Dad said, "I'll stay here and watch while you go home and have lunch. If you like, you can bring something back for me." He stayed all day. At the end, he watched them count the fronds and declare the winner. Dad was delighted with the victory dance. He said, "If we took this to Sydney, we'd make a fortune".

TROBRIAND WOMEN CARRY everything on their heads from their earliest years. It could be as heavy as a 4 gallon drum of kerosene or a very large suitcase or a bucket of water that they went to the pump to collect for their families. At times, the load was too heavy for one person to lift so two other girls would lift it up onto her head and be prepared to lift it off when they arrived at their destination. This was all part of being a Trobriand woman. It was their pride and dignity.

When I was behind a group of girls, I would marvel at the strength of their backs and necks and the beauty in their bodies. I remember attending a meeting where such practices were condemned by outsiders. When you live with a tribal people, you come to appreciate the values and customs which are theirs and not yours.

At harvest time everyone had the obligation to gather the yams and bring them to the village. The yams would be put in an inverted cone shape in the garden.

Conical piles of yams, Trobriand Islands. (Image courtesy JT Goddard.)

If you didn't help, you didn't have the right to eat. At midday on Friday when we finished classes, we would tell the children that we would drive them home in the truck so they would be in time to help. By the time the truck was ready, the children had all left, taking all kinds of short cuts through the bush to get there in time to be part of the harvest.

Students began leaving the Trobs after Grade 6 for high school. But when they returned they felt they shouldn't eat any yams because they hadn't helped during the harvest. So when the children went off to secondary school in Alotau and I was 17 kilometres away at Hagita, the people on the Trobs had to make a decision. They decided that the children who went away to school and couldn't take part in the harvest, could still eat because they are doing something the people wanted them to do. Higher education was greatly prized by the Trob people.

Radio Milne Bay was the local radio station. The students at Hagita were given their own radio session every Sunday evening. The radio people would come to the school and the children would speak in their language so that the people on the different islands would all understand them. The Trob students talked. Next morning all the parents came to the mission station at Gusaweta. They said that their children were dying. They hadn't been given any food to eat.

The parish priest who was there said that it couldn't be true. If it was true, the priests and Sisters at Hagita would have told us. The parents insisted that the children had said on the radio session the previous evening that they hadn't had any food for weeks. The parish priest got onto the mission radio and asked Hagita to explain. It turned out that the Trob children had not eaten yams for weeks. They'd eaten rice, sweet potatoes, fish, bread and greens, but they had not eaten yams. Food for the Trobriand Islanders meant yams. They had said on the radio that they were dying because they had no food but it was because they had no yams. It's like you haven't had your favourite food for weeks and you are just dying to eat it again.

A priest who worked on the Trobs for years used to say,

"If you're not interested in yams, don't come to the Trobriand Islands."

The culture around the yams was a wonderful thing – the planting, the havesting, the celebration after the harvest, the big *Milamala* feast that was hosted by the village with the biggest harvest. The whole year was centered around the yam.

Decorated yam house, Trobs. (Image courtesy JT Goddard)

The Trobs was about the only area in Milne Bay that had this depth of culture. Even now I know that yams continue to be a very important part of Trobriand Island culture. In Port Moresby, you know where the Trobriand Islanders live because of the yams growing up the sticks in the gardens. When somebody dies, the body is taken back to the Trobs. Family members return later for the sagali – the feast for the dead – at harvest time. Because of the nature of the islands, all coral islands, nothing else grows. They grow taro in the swamp area but there are never enough sweet potatoes. It's always the yam.

ON THE WEEKENDS, we'd go out as often as we could to the different inland villages to visit the children's parents. In 1970 when the government system started, we had to start having P&C (Parents and Citizens) meetings as well as a Board of Management for each school. I called a meeting of the parents to tell them that because the government was now paying the teachers, we had to do some things the government asked. The first thing was creating a P&C and the second thing was establishing a Board of Management.

One man put up his hand and said to me, "Sister, you have run these schools for many years and you have done a very good job. Now, if you want us to come in and help you, we will. We will come and do what you want us to do. But let me tell you, it's only going to mean hard work and trouble for you." He just couldn't see how they could help. In the Trobs, the parents were so reachable so we had more to do with them than in other places. Everyone could walk from place to place in the Trobs. Some places on the mainland could be reached by road, like Daio. For others, a boat was needed. At Budoya, on Fergusson, except for two villages, a boat was needed to all other places.

Initially, there were big central primary schools in each area. Students would come in from outlying areas to attend. There would be a boarding school and the students were usually not able to get home at weekends. It would depend on boats and weather. In 1970 when the government and churches formed the National Teaching Service, day schools were set up in the smaller villages and the need for children to leave home while at primary school lessened.

An annual open day was a great feature of the school program. Parents would tell me they didn't know what to look for or what to do when they visited their child's classrooms. I told them, "Look at your children's books. If you see an X red cross, it's not good. If you see a √ tic, then your child is doing good work. Then they would come in and go through their child's books and when they saw the Xs and say in local language, 'very bad, very bad' or they would saw the √s and say, 'very good, very good.'

They enjoyed the open days once they knew what they should do. The children enjoyed the open day as well because this showed their parents were interested in what they were learning. The Trob parents were very cooperative and supported us when we decided to do something. If we wanted to have a cultural day, the children would be dressed up to the nines. They would have the coloured banana skirts, the bagi, the armbands. The bagi were traditional necklaces made from red coral, smoothed into small stones and strung on a piece of fibre; the armbands were made from shells and beads.

THE STUDENTS on the Trobs really wanted to learn. One of the Sisters once taught the students three new words: *cannibal*, *nomad* and *kidnap*. One day a little old woman came onto the playground. She was all black. Her body was black with ashes. She was bent over, walking with a stick and looked like a witch. The children came running over to the convent. "Take the babies upstairs," they said, "and hide them." At that point in time we had several young children living with us as their parents were unable to look after them. We asked what it was about.

One of the girls explained, "She's a cannibal, a nomad and will kidnap the babies." We took the babies upstairs because the children were so agitated and worried that this woman would come and take the babies. This woman apparently was going to kidnap the babies, eat the babies, and then she was going to move onto the next village because she was a nomad. We kept the babies upstairs, sang to them, fed them lunch while the old woman circled the playground. Nobody touched her, talked to her or even went near her. Everyone just sat on the ground and watched her quietly. Then she went out through the gate and down the road.

THE GOVERNMENT MANAGED the hospital at Losuia on the Trobs. At Gusaweta, we treated small cuts and scratches. Every day we had a sort of medical session and I was the nurse. I put band aids on cuts and bruises. I used to write home to my parents and often there wasn't much to write about that they would understand. So I wrote home and told them about the kids who were sick and the fact we didn't have a lot to treat them with except for a few band aids.

The next thing was we had a visit from the Chief Medical Officer at Losuia. He was in charge of the government medical system on the Trobs. He wanted to know who had been complaining to Port Moresby or Canberra about lack of supplies. We hadn't complained to anyone so off he went to the United Church First Aid Post. No one there had been in touch with government officials either.

A couple of weeks later I received a letter from my

father in which was enclosed a letter from a Mr. Barnes, the Minister for External Territories for the Australian government. He wrote to apologize to my father that his daughter was working under such difficult circumstances in the Trobriand Islands. He was sorry that she did not have enough medical supplies for her school children and he would do something immediately to remedy the situation. It was me who was the cause of the trouble. The parish priest went to the medical centre at Losuia to confess that we had been the ones who had caused the trouble. We ended up with a great box of medical supplies which came from Port Moresby, specifically for Gusaweta.

THE TROBRIAND ISLANDS are very flat except for a small rise near Kaibola Beach. Every year, we would load all the Grade 6s onto the mission truck and head out to Kaibola for a picnic to celebrate the end of the year. When we came to that hill, or that mountain as the students called it, the students would make a terrible noise as we went up the hill and then more noise when we came down the other side. I mean you could easily walk up but for those Grade 6 students it was a real highpoint of their trip to Kaibola.

One time, Sister Margaret, who had been teaching at Gusaweta was preparing for the annual Christmas trip to Sideia. We usually took some girls with us but this time the boys asked to come as well. Sister Margaret told them if their parents gave permission they could come. So she had four boys with her as well as the girls. They spent the first night at Budoya on Fergusson Island. While they were having their evening meal, somebody came to the convent asking for Sister Margaret. She went to the door. The boys were there and one of them told her that they wanted to apologize. She asked them, "What have you done?"

One boy said, "When you gave us that lesson about mountains, we didn't believe you. But now we're here, we can really see true mountains. We believe you." Coming from the Trobs, they just couldn't imagine mountains and Fergusson was all mountains, many of them volcanic.

Every year, all the sisters from all the mission stations at Milne Bay would gather at Sideia for an annual retreat and relaxation.

The highlight was a day spent in Samarai shopping. We went between the two stores. We went into BPs to buy three large saucepans for the mission. The children did their own cooking and needed new ones. However, the saucepans only came as sets from the smallest to the largest. We explained to the salesman serving us that we didn't need the full set, we just wanted the largest saucepan from each set. "Oh, no," he said, "You can't do that. If you want the large saucepan, you have to buy the whole set. So if you want three, you'll have to buy three sets." We didn't want that so we left.

After a while we went back and the salesman we had talked to had gone for his lunch and another had taken his place. He asked us what we wanted and we explained again that we only wanted the three large saucepans at the bottom of the pile but we couldn't just buy the large saucepan. We had to buy the set. "Oh, no," said the new salesman. "You don't have to do that." He lifted out the three large saucepans and sold those to us. We dashed off with the saucepans before the other salesman came back from lunch.

IN THE 1980S, there were about 11,000 people on Trobs. Now the numbers have grown substantially. In 2009, I remember standing with a teacher on a verandah in Laluta, on the eastern end of the island. The teacher said to me, "Look down there." I looked and all I could see were bushes so that's what I told him.

He then told me, "You can't see any trees. All the trees have gone. We now use the land so often the trees don't have time to grow. The people cut the bushes and then replant." In my early days on Trobs the crops would be planted, harvested, and then the ground would lie fallow for 7 or 8 years. Now, because of the population growth, the land is often left alone only for a year.

After 7 years on the Trobs, I moved to Hagita. I lost my heart to the Trobriand Island people. They were so wild and willful but hungry for knowledge.

SIX
HAGITA, MILNE BAY PROVINCE
JANUARY 1973 - APRIL 1976

I WAS TRANSFERRED to Sacred Heart High School at Hagita to teach English. There was a convent at the school where I would stay. It was a 30 minute drive from Alotau, the new provincial headquarters, and only five minutes to the airport.

Hagita had only been going for a couple of years when I arrived. I loved it. I really and truly loved it. At Hagita, I was dealing with people on a different level. In the outstations I was in charge of the school. I was the boss and people did what I wanted them to do.

At the outstations, I had been dealing with Papua New Guinean teachers who didn't have much experience. They were good, they were fantastic teachers limited by their background and resources. Once they were shown what was possible, they became very creative. I felt I had to be the initiating inspiration after which they would do great things. I remember going to an outstation and seeing a really creative classroom. When I congratulated the teacher, he replied, "Sister, you taught me that." They remembered.

Now at Hagita, the teachers were inspiring and motivating me. When I went to Hagita I was dealing with expats, people from America, from England, from Australia, from Canada. They were trained teachers and they often inspired me.

I was teaching English, Social Science, Home Economics and Grade 7 maths. The teacher in charge of Maths was from the Trobs. He told me not to worry. If there was anything I didn't know he would come and teach my class. He was very paternal with me the whole time. When I saw the program it was what I had been teaching in Grade 6 - fractions, percentages, decimals. Now I was teaching it again in Grade 7. I didn't have any problem teaching it.

So now I had Grade 7 maths, Grade 7 and 8 English, which I really enjoyed, Social Science and Home Economics with the girls. I read *Around the World in 80 Days* with a Grade 8 class. We had a marvellous time with that book. The inspector came to my English class while we were doing *Around the World in 80 Days*. He said for an activity I could divide the class into groups and ask each group to draw a comic strip of a certain part of the book. We did it.

They had a marvellous time, especially the boys who were creative. They just took over - everybody told them what to draw and they did it. All around the classroom we had the comic strips of the book. I remember the School Inspector went to the Home Economics class and told me that I needed a strainer for the sink. When I told him that I didn't have one he explained how his wife had made one by punching holes in the bottom of a jam tin and using that as her sink strainer. I did that to make him happy and the next time he came I got a good mark because I had a sink strainer!

I had my high school English class outside, reading

books in groups. I wandered from group to group. A boy stopped me and asked me what a particular word meant. I asked him to read the sentence it was in and he did. I suggested that he should be able to figure out the meaning using the other words in the sentence. He struggled so I eventually gave him the meaning, and he said, "Well, I would never have thought of that."

ONE OF THE big highlights was the week's long sports carnival that we had at Hagita. It would be held at a different school each time. There were four high schools that took part: Sacred Heart in Hagita, Cameron High School in Alotau, Holy Name Girls' High School in Dogura, and Martyrs High School (only boys) in Popondetta.

I was in charge of providing morning tea for all the guests. I made these fancy little bread rolls. I overheard a man tell another teacher to eat the rolls because he said they were the best thing he had tasted in his life. I was right there and I was as proud as punch.

The girls from Holy Name were very dominant. They didn't take anything from the boys, they knew what they wanted. At Hagita the boys were the ones who said what was to be done. Whatever the boys wanted the girls did. If the boys said they were going to have a new uniform the girls made them. They got along wonderfully together but the boys were the dominant force. Even in the classroom the boys took the lead.

Those amazing girls from Dogura came to Hagita. They did just what they wanted. The boys would say that they didn't do it that way. The Dogura girls would say that that was the way they would do it. Our girls learnt that they had to be more dominant, more assertive with the boys. It was a great time for students and teachers. We had a quiz every night and Hagita won that year. There was organized sports, traditional dancing and marching. As each school marched around the oval they were judged. It was a really splendid time for them — a whole week of being together.

JUST BEFORE INDEPENDENCE, Michael Somare, who became the first Prime Minister after Independence, visited Hagita. The boys creatively adapted a traditional dance to celebrate Independence Day. Michael Somare asked them to perform the dance at the National Independence Day celebrations in Port Moresby. The boys travelled to Port Morseby on the *Morning Star* and enjoyed performing in public.

I was at Hagita for Independence Day on September 15th, 1975. It rained and rained and rained in Milne Bay. Everyone went to Alotau to watch the celebrations. Somebody had to stay home and mind the school so I did. During the morning we received word that the mother of one of the girls from Rossel Island had died.

It is amazing how things happen. At about lunchtime two of the girls came back to Hagita because they said there was nothing to see as it was raining and everybody was getting covered in mud. One of the girls was the daughter of the woman who had died. I had to break the sad news to her. That was my contribution to Independence Day.

THROUGHOUT MY TIME AT HAGITA, we had movie nights and showed a variety of films to the students. The mission had a film called *The March of the Wooden Soldiers,* now known as *Babes in Toyland*. It starred Stan Laurel and Oliver Hardy who worked for the toy maker. There was Bo-Peep and TomTom and the Bogeyman and the Three Pigs and The Old Woman who lived in the Shoe. It had all these nursery rhyme characters in it.

During most films we had to tell the children, "Keep quiet, keep quiet, listen to what they are saying." They couldn't hear, or couldn't understand the English or weren't interested so there was a murmur going on all the time. But when *The March of the Wooden Soldiers* was on, there wasn't a sound in the room. While the stars would be saying their part, the children would be mouthing the words. They knew the script off by heart.

The woman in the shoe couldn't pay her rent so Mr. Barnaby, who was the Bogeyman, said he was going to take her daughter, Bo-Peep instead. Finally, Bo-Peep and her mother agreed that Bo-Peep would marry Mr. Barnaby. But Mother Hubbard went to him and begged him not to take Bo-Peep. He said to her, "Woman, you're a fool." At which point all the children watching the film said, "Woman, you're a fool." They had seen it so many times. If there was nothing to do on a Saturday night and you asked them what they wanted to do, they would say "Watch Bo-Peep." It was a great film!

Another film we had was *Mary Poppins*. I said to Tom, one of the students, "Tom, we are going to watch *Mary Poppins* tonight. It is a lovely film." He told me he had seen it before and that she had arrived on an umbrella. He wondered if she was going to come on the umbrella when he watched it again. I told him yes and he said he thought she might. Some students couldn't grasp the concept of films, that there were actors playing roles. The films were so real to the students.

A visiting sister showed us *The Joyful Mysteries of the Rosary*. These films were about the early life of Jesus. There was the one about Jesus being lost after being in the temple. In the film, Mary and Joseph were walking through Jerusalem looking for their 12 year old son. Some soldiers came up to them. One of the soldiers asked, "Why are you out at night? You are breaking curfew." Joseph explained that they had lost their son. The soldier replied, "You will need to go home now and search again in the morning." As he said this, he put his hand on Mary's shoulder. As this happened, Joseph as well as every student watching it in the dining hall said, "Take your hand off her." It was amazing. It was all so real to them.

After 3 ½ years at Hagita, I was transferred to Alotau and became the Diocesan Education Secretary.

SEVEN

ALOTAU, MILNE BAY PROVINCE

APRIL 1976 - DECEMBER 1979; JANUARY 1990 -
DECEMBER 2001

ORIGINALLY, each of the religious denominations in PNG, Anglican, Catholic, Lutheran, and United, had its own education system with a government education department controlling all government schools. In 1970, the bishops from the four denominations decided they were unable to continue operating the schools themselves.

At that stage, the government school teachers were on a fortnightly wage, and received a leave fare every two years. The teachers at church schools were still being paid using the barter system. Every week they would receive a bottle of kerosene, a bar of soap, a tin of meat, and some rice, sugar and tea from the church in their community. At Christmas, the wives were given a supply of material to make clothes for their families. They were receiving no wage.

The bishops decided that they could no longer take responsibility for schools and that the government would have to take responsibility for the education of all children in Papua New Guinea. The government realized this was an impossible task for them. It was at this time that the National Education System and the Unified Teaching

Service were established. The church agencies would retain control of their schools with religious education having a central role in the daily operation of the school.

Each church agency would be responsible for the preparation and publication of its own religious education material. The religious lessons would form part of the ordinary daily timetable. The church agency representative would be a member of the Provincial Education Board and a member of board committees, such as student selection and teachers' appointments committee. Each church would be fully responsible for the establishment of their own central teacher training college. The government would pay staff wages and provide all necessary materials. The government didn't have the resources to fully take over the operation of the church schools.

AFTER ONE YEAR as Diocesan Education Secretary, this position was localized, and I became the Diocesan Christian Education Coordinator. We had 42 schools scattered around 14 different islands. I was responsible for visiting these schools and assisting the teachers. In the mid 70's we started a monthly school magazine called *Sail On*.

It was small, 16 pages, but it carried on for about 20 years. At one time it was the longest continuous running magazine in Papua New Guinea. It contained provincial education news, ideas and requests sent in by schools, school news, letters from readers, teaching hints, lives of prominent people such as Mandela and Anne Frank, and something on the saints of the month. If it was May, it was the month of Mary; October, the month of the Rosary; Easter time – all the stories of the resurrection. I took over in 1976 and kept it going until I left in 1984. Sister Delia continued until I returned in 1990. On my return, I continued with the publication until 2001. It had a wide distribution in Milne Bay and across Papua New Guinea. Although the magazine kept me busy, the school visits were the most important part of my work.

I remember going to a school at Horbuk. When I got off the boat the children were all lined up to welcome me, with the head teacher who was from Madang. He took me to sign the visitor's book but before I opened it, he asked, "Sister, I would like you to guess who the last visitor was to sign our guest book."

I guessed, "Father Tony, the parish priest." No, that wasn't who it was. "The school inspector." It wasn't him either. Then I asked, "Did you have any special visitors?" No, that hadn't happened. Finally we looked. The last person to have signed the book was me. That's how important my visit was to them as often it was the only visit they had from the outside in 12 months. The first thing the teachers asked me when I arrived was whether I had brought this month's *Sail On* magazine. It was a connection with the outside world. It helped them with their teaching and had stories of what other schools were doing. In turn, they sent in stories of what they were doing.

Across from Horbuk was the island of Sabra where we had a school at the village of Maho. Truly the most beautiful setting of any school I visited. From the classroom you stepped out onto a wide stretch of bright green grass. That led down to beautiful white sand. From there, you went into crystal blue water. In the evening, I would watch the moon rise out of the water. It was magnificent! In the morning, I would watch the red sun rise from the sea.

The mission boat that had dropped me off at Horbuk had returned to Nimoa. It would come for me at the end of the week. When I was ready to go across to Maho, a large sea going canoe came for me. The crew told me to sit on a box in the bottom of the canoe, which meant I couldn't see anything. I asked them if I could sit up higher and they gave me another box. The pandanus leaf sail was unfurled and we just flew across the bay to Maho. It was one of the loveliest trips I ever had.

I mainly visited primary schools but would include secondary schools and vocational schools that were on the islands. In the last week of the school year, just before the Christmas holidays, I would conduct inservice training sessions for the teachers.

When I visited schools, I went to each one of the classes and watched the teachers give a religion lesson. At the end of the lesson, I would talk to the children. Usually, I would get them to ask me questions. They could ask me anything. I'd say, "Please don't ask my mother and father's name or how old I am, because everybody asks me that. See if you can think of something new."

I remember one little boy at Rossel. He put up his hand and asked, "What means *Rebecca*?"

I replied, "I'm not sure, but when I go back home, I'll find out and I'll let you know." I could have done it there and then if I had thought of it. The Good News Bible tells the meaning of names of all the people in the stories. When I returned to Alotau, I found out that *Rebecca* means - 'the one who carries water', because she had carried water for the camels of Abraham's servant. I wrote a letter to this little boy and told him that Rebecca means, 'the one who carries water'.

About 3 years later, I was walking down the path at Sacred Heart High School, Hagita, when this Grade 7 boy came up to me and said, "Can I ask you a question?"

I said, "Yes."

He asked, "What means *Rebecca*?"

I replied, "You tell me."

He smiled. "The one who carries water." He had come in from Primary School to Secondary School and he had remembered.

Another time, we were doing initials, like CBC. CBC means Catholics Bishops Conference.

The children told me to write PNGBC on the board. "Try this one," they challenged me.

"It means Papua New Guinea Banking Corporation," I said.

The students exclaimed, "No!"

I said, "Yes. PNGBC - Papua New Guinea Banking Corporation."

Again, the students shouted, "No!"

"Well then, tell me, what does it mean?" I asked.

They replied, "Papua New Guinea Baptist Church."

If they could tell me something I didn't know that was a real red letter day for them. I loved these sessions with the children. They came alive when they could ask things. The visit always ended with a teachers' meeting and some in service training — touching on a topic that they had requested. That was until the boat came and I moved on to the next school.

ONE TIME I went to Maho early in the year. Because of transport difficulties, no teachers had arrived at the school. Sister Stella, who was home on holidays, had taken on the teaching of the whole school. I prolonged my stay to help her. After a while, the teachers began to drift in, so Stella and I left and the teachers carried on.

One day, I arrived late at Budoya. The school inspector had begun the National Teachers' In-service Training Program. He was talking to the teachers, so I sat in the back of the classroom. Written on the blackboard was: T is not T and L is not L. For a while, I puzzled over what this meant. Then I asked the teacher beside me to explain. He whispered, "Talking is not teaching and listening is not learning." In other words, the children could be listening to you but because they might be thinking of other things, they weren't learning anything. If you hadn't prepared your lesson you were talking, not teaching.

I often travelled alone on one of the mission boats on their regular trips to the islands. I usually stayed with a teacher or in a house they had prepared for me. I took my mat but never took a pillow because I could always manage without one. A pillow was too big and bulky to carry. I once went into a house and the teacher had everything ready for me – a lovely mat and blanket but no pillow. She explained, "Sister, I didn't get a pillow because Father Moore said that whenever you leave Budoya you never take a pillow."

I had been asked to go to Rossel Island and stay there for a while because Sister Caritas, a Papua New Guinean Sister from Nimoa, the neighbouring island, had been left on her own. One Sister had gone for a meeting and another had had to go to the mainland for medical treatment. I ended up being there for six weeks. Each morning I went down to the school and asked if there was anything I could do. I was given classes to teach so I was busy during the day.

Sister Caritas was a lovely person, but she had no great conversational skills. She loved playing canasta. Every night, that's what we'd do. Father English, the priest at Rossel, would come over to the convent for meals. He was a great talker and liked to argue with everyone. I enjoyed sparring with him. Every fortnight, he would leave to visit outstations at different points of the island.

One day two men from Cameron Secondary School in Alotau arrived on a government boat and walked up to the Mission station. I remember that I talked and I talked and I talked. Later, I couldn't believe it as at that time, I wasn't a great talker. After they left, I thought to myself that they probably thought I was mad. I was excited because it was the first real company, real conversation, I'd had with anybody in six weeks.

ROSSEL ISLAND WAS A LOVELY PLACE, surrounded by a reef. Walking there at low tide was just like walking in a miniature Japanese garden. But we had to leave the protected harbour at Jinjo and sail outside the reef to visit the next school. Once we moved out of the passage and through the opening in the reef, the waves were as high as mountains.

We were on our way to East Point, and had only gone a little way when the engine suddenly stopped. You know, in the Bible it says, "Walls of water to the right and walls of water to the left." That's all I could think of. These huge walls of water were coming down in front of us, and huge walls of water were rising up behind us. We were climbing up one side and sliding down the other. It was really, really terrifying.

All the canoes from the village came out and waited on the calm side of the reef, thinking the boat would be thrown onto the reef and they would be able to save the passengers. The women on board were screaming and screaming. I started saying the Hail Mary: "Hail Mary, full of grace the Lord is with you" at the top of my voice, hoping to stop their screaming. Nobody answered. They all kept screaming, except for one little boy. He kept saying, "Holy Mary, Mother of God, Holy Mary, Mother of God". Suddenly I said, "Hail Mary full of grace" and he answered in Rossel language. He was so frightened he couldn't think of the English. Eventually the crew got the engine going and demanded, "We turn around and go back to Jinjo."

Father disagreed, "We go straight on and turn into the next inlet." We kept going until the engine stopped. The noise started all over again with me praying, the little boy answering in Rossel language, and the women screaming. Eventually, the engine started again. The crew didn't ask anything, they just turned the boat around and headed back to Jinjo. As we pulled into the wharf, the women jumped off and started walking to East Point, which was a long way away, but they would never get back on that boat.

WHENEVER THE BISHOP WAS TRAVELLING, I would go along. Once, we left Nimoa, which was the Mission station before Rossel. We sailed down the east side of Sudeste (also known as Tagula Island) and anchored for the night at Rambusco. Because of the weather, we stayed there for 2 days.

On the 3rd day, the Bishop said, "We're going to Rossel." It was incredibly frightening. The bishop said, "Get on the bunk and stay there." That's all I wanted to do. If I was going to go to the bottom of the sea, I'd rather be on the bunk than be fighting outside.

Another time, I was coming back from Nimor to Alotau by plane. Father Sam's home was Nimor Island and he had just been ordained there. I had been on Rossel Island so I had come by boat to Nimor for the ordination and was now returning to Alotau by plane. As we flew, we saw this huge white cloud in front of us. The pilot flew straight into the cloud. It was like hitting a brick wall. The plane shuddered all over. Anybody who didn't have a seat belt on, including the person sitting next to the pilot, and the one sitting behind me, landed on the floor. The plane went up and down and round and back. It went anywhere it wanted to. The pilot told us afterwards, the more he positioned the joystick, to take the plane up, the more the nose went down to the ground. The plane was like a piece of paper being tossed about inside this cloud.

Suddenly, we came out of the cloud. There in front of us was a waterfall. The pilot just had time to turn the plane. We were so close, I'm sure the wings were wet from the spray of the waterfall on them. Then the pilot announced, "I've never been in this area before. Can anyone tell me where we are?" Everybody looked out of the windows to try and find some landmark. We all started calling out names.

After a while, Father Jim Moore spoke up. "I think we've just passed over the United Church Bible School on Normandy Island. If I am right, there's an airstrip just ahead of us. Can we turn around and go over this place again?" The pilot said, "We haven't got enough fuel even to be able to turn around. Let's hope the airstrip is in front of us." We went on a little further and there was the airstrip on Normandy Island.

When we landed, everyone was happy to get off the plane. Across the bay was Salamo, the central United Church mission station. The pilot told Father Moore, "I have enough fuel to take the Sisters across to Salamo for the night."

Father Moore replied, "Nobody wants to go anywhere. We will all stay here for the night." We had pork to eat because we were bringing it from Father Sam's ordination feast to Port Moresby. There was bread that one of the Sisters had baked because of a baker's strike in Port Moresby and there was plenty of cake left over from the feast as well. We took the axe out of the plane's emergency kit to cut up the cake and the bread. The men's razors were used to slice the pork.

That night, the women slept in the plane while the men sat up in a little shed listening to England and Australia playing cricket. The next morning a plane flew in from Alotau with fuel. The ones who were going to Alotau left on that plane. The ones going to Moresby stayed on the original plane. It had been a frightening experience.

IN MY LAST year as Diocesan Christian Education Coordinator, I was invited to go to the centenary celebration at Dogura. Again, the weather was frightful. I climbed on the back deck of this boat and sat in the corner. I don't think I moved for the whole journey. Nobody knew where Dogura was so we just kept on going further and further along the coast of Papua New Guinea. Suddenly one woman said we had gone too far. We had been on board for a day and a night. The captain turned around and we went back. Eventually we found Dogura.

On the return trip, it was just as rough. When I got on the boat, a strange woman had taken charge. She was a fly in, fly out teacher. She would fly from Alotau to the mines to teach and then fly back to be with her husband. She told me to have something to eat, then get onto a bunk and not to move. I had no objections. I had something to eat and was very happy to have a bunk to climb onto. It was certainly better than the corner of the back deck!

Later, she came along and asked me if a little girl could sleep with me. Of course I said yes and the little one climbed up on the bunk. We held on to each other to stay on the bunk. It was a time when I was wearing the veil but I had no veil on in the bunk. The little girl kept rubbing her hands through my hair and repeating "Ahhh, it is so soft, so soft."

I thought that was great. It was the first positive thing anybody had ever said about my hair. My hair was so thin and so straight you couldn't do anything with it. My mother used to put it in rags when I was a little girl. I would sleep all night in these rag curls. They would stay in place all day. Mum would take them out in the afternoon as we were going to a party. I would have these lovely little curls. But by the time I reached the front door I had straight hair.

There was no way anybody could ever say anything positive about my hair. Now here was this little one saying to me, "Oh, it's so soft. It is so soft." She was so used to the tight curly hair of the Papua New Guineans. You couldn't possibly run your fingers through their hair. There she was running her fingers through what seemed like a magnificent silk cord.

WHILE MY VISITS to schools out east usually involved some form of drama, those to schools on Fergusson and Goodenough were much more peaceful. The ten schools scattered around Fergusson could all be reached either by walking or a short trip on an outboard motor dinghy. Gerard, the very pleasant outboard motor operator at Budoya, was always ready and willing to take me out.

The closest out station school from Budoya was a short boat trip followed by a steep mountain climb. The school children would come down to carry the cargo. Once everything was equally shared, off we went. We came to a crevice spanned by a lone coconut log bridge. The children, loaded as they were, seemed to dance across. With a helper both before and behind me. I crept across that log not daring to look further than my feet. After the school visit I was no better on the return trip but my guides were gentle and patient and steered me safely across.

The next school, Basima, was right on the coast. The only problem was getting enough time between the waves to get high and dry onto the land. Much to Gerard's amusement I usually managed to get a soaking.

Basima beach had no sand. It was made of large, smooth pebbles. These were thrown up by the incoming waves and then pulled down as the water went out. They were worn smooth and shiny from the constant movement. Of an evening I liked to sit on a pile of stones, listen to the sounds and wait for the moon to rise. One night two young boys came and sat on either side of me.

"What are you doing?" they asked.

"I'm praying." I replied.

"Can we stay with you?" they requested.

I responded, "If you remain still and silent."

So the three of us sat and watched as the moon rose up out of the ocean. When it was high enough in the sky I said, "We can talk now if you like."

They had been silent with me so now I tried to answer their many questions.

Goodenough posed the least problems. All six schools could be reached by walking along the well worn beach track. On my first visit Fr. John told me the walk from the main Government station at Bolobolo to Mataita was a gentle walk over undulating hills. With my companion as guide we set off. We walked up and down, up and down hills as steep as camels' humps. Exhausted I stopped to cut up a pineapple which we shared then set off again. Up and down. At the top of each hill as I saw another in front of me, my companion said, "Only one more, Sister. Only one more."

There was no way this fellow could count!

Finally we met a man going in the opposite direction. He was walking towards Bolubolu.

"Are you going to Bolubolu?" I asked.

"Yes," he replied.

I asked, "Do you know Fr. John?"

"Yes," he said.

"Please tell Fr. John, Sister Helen is not moving until a boat comes," I said tiredly.

We crossed one more hill and there was the school with students and teachers waiting with a welcome. When my visit was over the boat at Budoya, the *St. Paul*, had cargo to bring to Bolubolu. On its way, it called in to get me so I missed the undulating hills on the way home.

The school in the opposite direction from Bolubolu was Kalauna. Fr. John offered me the use of his motorbike for that visit.

"Just turn left at the school sign and you will soon see the school," he explained before I left. "No chance of missing the school sign as it is so clear and bright."

I turned left and went on along a narrow path. Then up a steep hill along a path that became narrower and narrower. Suddenly I realized just how high I was and how impossible it was for a school to be way up there. I stopped the bike as a fellow came round the bend in front of me.

"Where is the school?" I asked.

"Down there," he replied as he pointed way down the

mountain to a set of very small buildings tucked into a corner I had passed soon after turning in at the school sign. Somehow in that narrow space my helper managed to turn the bike for me. Now I was facing the opposite direction so I got on and started the engine.

The bike took off. It flew down that mountain with me just managing to keep the tyres on the narrow track. The bike had no brakes but had a will of its own. When I reached the school grounds I carefully guided the bike to the left and then let it run until it died. It went round and round in circles gradually going slower and slower until finally coming to a halt. In the meantime the children had come running out of class and formed their own circle around me. They cheered as I went round and round. As the engine died there was a great roar and much clapping that all had ended well.

I managed to walk to the three other schools on Goodenough.

ON LAND or sea travel could mean some form of drama. Although I can't recall any such excitement when visiting the six schools on Normanby Island. The four schools where I needed a boat had easy landing areas while the other three were reached along pleasant beach or bush walks.

There were other schools like those along the rough Molima Coast on the west side of Fergusson. The lone school on Sim Sim Island, which was just a dot in the middle of the Coral Sea, yet there were children living there needing education. Sanaroa and Basilaki Islands stood alone. The hardest of all to reach was Woodlark, a two day boat trip in open seas from the Trobs. In the course of my time as Diocesan Christian Education Coordinator I managed to visit all of them several times. It was a wonderful experience meeting teachers ready to go to such isolated spots to teach children. The students were so eager to learn and parents willing to sacrifice so much if it meant their children could move away and learn something new.

I enjoyed the time I spent in Milne Bay both as a teacher and then as the Diocesan Education Secretary but my time there had come to an end. I was to become the Postulant Mistress on Yule Island and was going to enter a new phase of my working life.

EIGHT

YULE ISLAND

JUNE 1984 - DECEMBER 1989

I WENT to Yule Island to be Postulant Mistress. The women who arrived were young, often between the ages of 17 and 23. They came to see if they really wanted to live a religious life.

Postulant is a word that means 'I see'. A postulant was a young woman coming to see if this was what she wanted. If she stayed, a two year novitiate followed the postulate. At the end of the novitiate, the novices made their first vows.

At the time, Sister Patricia was the Novice Mistress. Sister Claire who came from the Trobriand Islands, and with whom I'd worked in the Trobs, was in charge of the cooking and sewing. She also helped me with the postulants. We taught Liturgy, Church History, the study of the Old Testament, and the history of our congregation.

All the novices were from Papua New Guinea while I was there. However, at one stage, we did have an South African postulant. We had a large group of Australian Sisters working in South Africa, and a young woman with whom they had worked, wanted to enter, to become a postulant. At the time, South Africa hadn't set up their own formation centre. They asked if she could join us. She came and did her Postulancy and Novitiate at Yule Island and then returned to South Africa. She added great life and colour to the Novitiate program.

Before they came to Yule Island, the young women had been in contact with a Sister in their own area for a year or two. Sometimes, the young women would live with the Sisters for a while. Often, one of the Sisters would take the young woman under her wing, and tell her about the congregation and what it meant to be a Sister, what work prayer meant in religious life, and what relationships with the people meant in our own lives.

If the Sister thought this young woman was suitable, she sent her name and contact information to the Vocation Directress who would ask that the young woman write a letter to the Provincial asking to become a Sister. The Provincial with her Council would consider the application. They would either accept or reject her. The young women who came thus already had a relationship with some of the Sisters.

Several of those who came changed their minds. I can remember saying the rosary with one postulant. When we were finished, she said to me, "What do you call somebody who studies flowers?"

I said, "I think a horticulturist."

She replied, "When I finish my novitiate training that's what I'll do, I'll go to the university and study horticulture."

I said to her, "You know, you didn't really come here to decide if you're going to go to the university. You've come here to decide if you want to be a Sister." Eventually she left.

Another lovely one was Carmelina. Carmelina was a

beautiful person. One day she came to me and said, "This is not for me."

I said, "That's okay. That's what you came here to find out — if this is for you." Carmelina left, got married, had a beautiful baby boy.

I had to say to a young woman from Manus, "We don't feel you are suitable. We think this is not what you're meant to be. We think you're meant to be with your people, helping them in another way but not in this way." We could see that she wasn't really cut out for religious life but she returned home and did great work in her village as a Catechist.

IN MY FIRST group I had eight postulants, three of whom returned home before making their final vows. One woman made her first vows, but before she made her final vows, she decided to leave. As part of their formation, the novices would spend six weeks living in a community, often an isolated outstation. They could be on an island or on the top of a mountain. There they would have a taste and a feel of what religious life would be like. They needed to ask themselves, "Can I live this way?"

Every young Sister should have this experience before she makes her first vows, her final vows and then her final commitment. When I made my final vows, it was three years after my first vows, but now it can be as long as nine years. Most Sisters make their final vows after six years. One Sister from my first group, when she had completed her first three years, said, "I want to make my final vows now. I know what I want. I don't want to wait any longer. I want to make my final vows now." She later became Postulant Mistress herself.

There are several Sisters that stand out in my mind. Antoinette was a Secondary School teacher who entered with four other young women. One was a Primary School teacher and the other two didn't have a great education but we accepted them. I always admired Antionette because she knew the answers to a lot of the questions I was asking because of her educational background but she never rushed in. She always waited and gave the others a chance to give their opinions, their ideas. If she did give an answer she never made them feel small. She never had the attitude that she was smarter than they were.

Sister Paula had polio as a child on Goodenough Island. One of the Brothers found her in the village. She was getting around, hopping on her good leg. He asked the people if he could take her to Sideia, where the Sisters would look after and help her. The Sisters did as much as they could for her. They contacted a doctor in Australia who agreed to look at her leg. Paula went to Australia. While she was there, she met Pope Paul VI. There's a beautiful picture of Paula with a big white bow on the top of her head standing in front of him. She stood and talked with him. A Papua New Guinean nurse called Elizabeth was with her.

Paula went first to her village after her trip to Australia. She then came into Sideia to complete her primary education. From there she went to Sacred Heart, Hagita, and finished her secondary education. She became a secretary in the Mission Office in Sideia. One day, she approached Sister Antonius and said she wanted to be a Sister. Sister Antonius asked, "Paula, do you want to become a Sister because you have only one good leg?"

Paula was really shocked. She said, "No! No! I don't want to be a Sister because I only have one good leg. I'm going to be a Sister because I've seen how you people live, and I want to be like you." Paula was fantastic. She never used her disability to avoid anything.

At the Novitiate, we walked up to the main mission station for Mass every morning. One of the novices would come up to me and carry my prayer books. They'd come up to Paula and say, "Paula, I'll carry your prayer book." They'd carry Paula's prayer book so she could move easily on her crutches.

One day, we had a fire so all the postulants and novices rushed to get the great big galvanized tubs that one of the Brothers had made. They were like those big old tubs that were used to do the washing in or have a bath in earlier times. They had handles on both sides and were now filled with water to put out the fire. When the fire was out, we walked back to the Novitiate. I saw Paula carrying this great big tub, hopping along on her one good leg. I couldn't help thinking, "Can I carry your prayer books?" yet no one thought of saying, "Can I carry your tub for you?"

Paula would go out to collect and chop the wood. She took her turn in the kitchen and laundry. Paula was involved in everything. Paula eventually went to Australia, and had her leg straightened. A steel rod was inserted from her hip to her ankle, and she was fitted with a special shoe. This gave her greater mobility. Paula has always been a role model for others with disabilities.

AS POSTULANT MISTRESS, I was dealing closely with people who enjoyed learning. We had a great time. We had classroom sessions from 9:00 am to 10:00 am, from 11:00 am to 12:00 pm, and again from 2:00 to 4:00 pm. This wasn't just a classroom relationship. It was closer than that.

It was a relationship with young women who wanted to be what I was – a Sister. I kept asking them, "Is this what you really want to be? Is this what you really want to do?"

I always had them do a project on Father Jules Chevalier who started our congregation so that they would know something about him. We read and acted the story of his life, and then they would choose the parts of his life that they wanted to write about in their project books. They carried those books with them long after they left Yule Island.

The Novitiate is situated on a cliff. There is a dreadful descent down the front — an awkward set of cement steps. They're sloping forward, so it is easy to fall over going down. You have to climb like a mountain goat coming up. At the bottom of the stairs is a beautiful sandy beach called St. Patrick's. It's nearly all eroded now by the sea. But in my time it was a beautiful beach for swimming. There were also many mango trees. When I saw no one eating mangoes or swimming, I suggested that the Postulants do so during the break from 10 to 11 o'clock in the morning. That idea was well received.

During Lent, I used a book that gave us something to do each day. This particular day it suggested making bread and watching it rise or fishing. Both activities required waiting. You can't make the bread rise in a hurry. You can't make the fish hurry up and come. Everyone decided to go fishing at 10 o'clock when we had our break. I went down at 10 o'clock and threw in my line. Suddenly I saw a deadly black and white sea snake. If you are bitten, you are dead in three minutes.

I yelled and screamed, "Help! Come quickly." All the Postulants saw me from the top of the hill. They told me later they thought I had caught a big fish and needed help bringing it ashore. So, one ran to get a bag, another ran to get a bush knife, another ran to get something else. Nobody came to me. I was still screaming because the huge thing was coming down the side of the rock, while the Postulants were all moving so slowly. They all arrived and said, "Where's the fish? Where's the fish?"

I shouted, "There's no fish, but there's a snake!" and I pointed to the coral rock. The snake was sliding into a hole. Hedwig dashed over to the rocks and eventually got there just in time to cut off the snake's tail as it disappeared into the hole. The snake lived to see another day. The next year we would make bread and watch it rise. It would be safer.

ONE MORNING, we decided to put the large fishing net out. That evening, we had tea on the beach. Before we ate, the Postulants decided it was time to pull the net in. Hedwig dived in first to pull the net out. "It's so heavy, I can't pull it. Somebody come and help me."

One of the Postulants went to help her, and then asked for everyone to come and help. Everyone went to help. I thought they were joking. They pulled and tugged at this fishing net. When it finally came out it was alive with a whole school of fish. We had a marvellous time, taking the fish out of the net, cleaning them and putting them into plastic bags to freeze. We cooked some over the fire and had a delicious meal. We had a great time.

There were lots of outdoor activities such as our day on the beach using the wide stretch of white sand to carve up the Promised Land for the twelve tribes of Judah. We celebrated the festivals of Harvest, Shelters, Atonement and Purim. We sang, danced and prayed the Psalm of the Exiles, by the rivers of Babylon. Everyone enjoyed these sessions and came to appreciate the beauty of God's relationship with the Chosen People.

It was a very enjoyable six years. It didn't have the stress and strain of the classroom or the demands of time. We could make our own timetable according to our needs. In addition, there were wonderful relationships that developed with these young women who arrived on Yule Island, not sure if they were in the right place.

YULE ISLAND IS in the Gulf of Papua. It's near Bereina, which is about 160 km from Port Moresby, the capital of Papua New Guinea. It is just a very small island, about ten minutes by outboard motor from the mainland.

It's where the Catholic Church began in Papua. In 1885, a priest by the name of Henry Verius landed on Yule Island with two Missionary of the Sacred Heart Brothers. Father Henry Verius celebrated Mass on the hill on July 4, 1885. In 1886, the first Sisters arrived. From Yule Island, the missionaries went east to Port Moresby and then further east to Milne Bay. They went across to the mainland to the Mekeo and Roro areas, then up into the Goilala and Southern Highland mountains. They went west up the rivers of the Gulf province. Yule Island is the very centre and birthplace of the Catholic Church in the whole of that southern area of Papua New Guinea.

Every year on the 4th July, Foundation Day on Yule Island, there's a great celebration. In 1985, just one year after I arrived, there were tremendous festivities to commemorate 100 years since the foundation of the Catholic Church in Papua New Guinea.

For a week, we had special masses with processions. We had concerts, traditional dancing and feasting. The NBC

(National Broadcasting Corporation) sent out a team to record what was happening. Sister Mary Paula had written a play that began with the birth of Jesus in Bethlehem, told of Father Chevallier's initiative and the missionaries coming to Yule Island. The climax was the ordination of the first Papuan priest, Father Louis Vangeke. While the play was being performed, the radio people asked Sister Mary Paula to explain what was happening. Because of her French accent, she passed the microphone to me. I was delighted to tell what was happening as the story unfolded.

It was really a wonderful time. We ran up and down that hill like mice. I don't know now how I did it. We ran up and down that hill where Father Verius had celebrated the first Mass many times. We ran up and down for Mass, and then up and down for processions.

Before coming to Yule Island, Sister Patricia Claire and I had attended a three months formator workshop at Bomana, just outside Port Morseby. One of the participants in the formation workshop, Sister Cecilia from the Solomon Islands, taught us the song, 'I believe in Angels'. We had these magnificent actions of waving our arms and turning and twisting and doing all kinds of movements to go with the song. We decided to teach the postulants and novices 'I Believe in Angels' and perform it at the Centenary celebrations. We needed special clothes for these angels. We wanted long white robes with wide flowing sleeves. A parish in Port Moresby sent over some robes and I made the rest. Wearing our new outfits, we all sang "I Believe in Angels". Everybody enjoyed it and thought it was marvellous. Every time we went anywhere, people would say to us, "Oh, sing 'I believe in Angels'."

The centenary gave people the opportunity to celebrate their Faith. The Archbishop of Port Moresby came to take part in the celebrations. He was to be the main celebrant at the Sunday Mass. Because of the heavy rain that had fallen, his small bus was stuck in the mud so he arrived late, but no one minded the delay.

YULE ISLAND IS a beautiful place for a Novitiate. There is much discussion as to where the Novitiate should be. It is now so difficult to get from Port Morseby to Bereina, where the boat takes everything across to Yule Island. There are fewer men on the island now, and only the Parish Priest at the mission station. The Yule Island Girls' Secondary School has moved over to the mainland. The vocational centre has closed. Now, there's only the primary school. It is going back to the very foundations when the Sisters first arrived.

But it is a perfect place for the formation of the young women who want to look at what it means to become a Religious. After six wonderful years there, I left to return to Milne Bay and resumed the role of Diocesan Religious Education Coordinator.

NINE

PORT MORESBY

JANUARY 2002 - DECEMBER 2009

AFTER MY SECOND stint as Diocesan Religious Education Coordinator, my first position in Port Moresby was Course Coordinator at Xavier Institute. The institute conducted courses related to religious life. I would organize ongoing formation courses for religious men and women. I also provided instruction for young religious men and women who were preparing to make their final vows.

Each week, I had to bring in a guest speaker from the nearby seminary to speak to students. The secretary of the Apostolic Nuncio came to talk on Canon Law, the laws governing religious life in the Catholic Church. Before he came, I told the participants, "When this man comes, you'll have to get matchsticks to hold your eyes open. As soon as he starts talking, you'll fall asleep. When anyone explains Canon Law, the audience goes to sleep." He came and nobody slept! Everybody was fascinated with what he had to say. He was so alive. He made it all so practical and meaningful for their own lives.

I learnt not to be afraid to ask people to come and speak. Different people came from other parts of Papua New

Guinea and Australia to speak and inspire. I was also called on to speak on several topics. Because many of the participants came from outside Port Moresby, I organized visits to places of interest, including Catholic schools. As visitors, we spoke to the students and engaged in discussions with them. It was an interesting year which I greatly enjoyed.

In 2002, I was asked to be the National Christian Education Coordinator (NCEC). This was a high point of my life because now I could travel the entire length of the country. Ah, fantastic! I visited 19 provinces. The only province I missed was the Northern Province because there were no Catholic schools there at that time.

EARLY IN MY term as NCEC the Education Department introduced Personal Development as a compulsory subject in all schools from Grade 5-12. The Bishops felt the material provided by the Education Department merely covered the biological and physical aspects of the human body. They wanted a holistic program which included moral and spiritual aspects of the human person. They approached me to prepare such a program that would help combat the HIV and AIDS epidemic that was sweeping over the country then.

I began with a teachers' handbook to be used in group inservices. In this first book, there was information on every kind of contraception with possible side effects. There was also a section on the Catholic Church's view with approved recommendations. The whole picture was given to the teachers but abstinence was stressed.

Over the years I had come to realize everyone seemed to know how a woman's body functions because every Health Clinic has charts on the wall explaining family planning, pregnancy and aspects of childbirth. Sister Marlene, one of our very competent nurses was heavily involved in the treatment of HIV and AIDS as well as being Tutor at St. Gerard's School of Nursing. She agreed to help me introduce the topic of the male body at an NCES and NCEC Workshop.

Sister Marlene gave an introductory talk, then announced everyone was to get into mixed sex working groups to identify the parts of the male body. One of the senior NCES came up to her and whispered, "Sister we can't get into mixed groups for this. We'll just get into groups of men and women." Sr. Marlene drew herself up to her full six foot height and announced in a booming voice, "We will get into mixed groups." No further objections! Everyone moved into mixed groups. At the end of the session, the NCES who had objected about the mixed groups came and told me when he went home he was going to explain to his wife all that he had learnt.

At another inservice training, whoever was supposed to come to teach the physical part of the human body failed to turn up. I discovered there was a nurse at the aid post so I asked her if she would she come and teach it for me. She was hesitant. I said, "Look, I'll be there. I know it, I just don't know how to present it properly because I'm not a nurse. If you need any help, just ask me. You can just look at me and I'll step in and add whatever is necessary."

She agreed. Later I found out her husband was one of the participating teachers. He disappeared from the group. He couldn't stay there while his wife gave such a presentation. I didn't know that until afterwards. I said to the other teachers, "Why wasn't he there?"

They said, "Sister, it was his wife, he couldn't be there."

Most of the participants were men. At the end of it, I

always asked if there were any questions? No, no questions. But then, one man put his hand up and asked a very simple question. It broke the ice and every hand in the class went up. Every man had a question. It was really beautiful how they had opened up.

THERE WERE many challenges in this position. A lot of time was spent traveling, but these visits showed the Provincial Catholic Education Secretaries and Catholic Education Coordinators how much their work was valued. It also gave me the opportunity to conduct inservice training on the new material. I wasn't waiting for people to come in once a year with their reports but was actually going to the provinces to see their reports put into action.

When it came to creating a personal development program for use in schools, I found it very difficult until I came in contact with a program created by Bishop Hugh Slattery for South African youth. I was given permission to adapt this material for the Papua New Guinean situation. Once I started and found extra sources of material, I really enjoyed creating this new program.

I didn't have a committee, it was just me, one woman doing the job.

I SECURED FUNDING to ensure the inservice training for the Catholic Education Secretaries and Christian Education Coordinators became a permanent annual occurrence. The participants came in every year for a week. Each year we explored different topics.

One year, it was Computer Programming. With great difficulty, I managed to obtain a laptop for each of the

Education Secretaries, and that was just not heard of. Usually, no charitable organization would finance anything that was moveable. They would finance desk computers, they would finance cupboards or anything that was secured in place, but they wouldn't finance anything could be just picked up and taken away. I was working with a lovely woman, who in the end, managed to convince her organization that laptops were the answer for the out stations.

The next year when their reports were submitted, many of them were on memory sticks and the reports were given as PowerPoint presentations.

Another initiative was to obtain funding so as to begin an annual inservice week for the principals of our Catholic secondary schools. Formerly, high schools had grade 7-10 and in the new format, secondary schools had Grades 8 -12. The principals had no special training for this situation. They went from classroom teaching to administration and teaching. I organized annual week long inservices for these principals and covered topics where they needed assistance to bridge the divide.

I had a wonderful time, creating material for students and teachers that was useful then and continues to play a role in the education system. At the end of 2009, my role ended and I began a new chapter of my life creating a literacy program.

TEN
MY OPUS
JANUARY 2010 - SEPTEMBER 2019

MY POSITION as National Christian Education Coordinator ended in December 2009. In January 2010, I was living in our convent at Boroko, wondering what I was going to do. A Sister from another congregation came along and said that there were some women up on the hill, where some Highlanders lived in a settlement, who would like to learn to read and write. I said, "That's good. You and I can start a literacy class." She agreed but became involved in other activities.

I decided to start a literacy class myself. I put a notice in the Sunday church bulletin saying that literacy classes would be held in the parish hall on Tuesdays and Thursdays from 9:00 am until 11:30 am. A couple of weeks later I went over to the parish hall to sit and wait. About half a dozen people straggled in. I started by singing the A, B, Cs and then moved to phonics and sounds. I hung phonetic charts on the walls.

Several weeks later, the Sister returned and commented, "Those women up on the hill are very disappointed because they haven't had any lessons."

I said, "We've been having lessons for about 4 weeks now. The women haven't come."

She explained that they had been waiting for me to come up to them.

I responded, "No way. I'm not taking charts and books and pencils up the hill every day. There's no shelter. They'll be blowing all over the place. If they want classes, they'll have to walk down the hill"

I never had any of that group of women in my class.

Most people who came lasted for the year. After a while, Moses turned up. Moses was a balding, grey haired man who always wore a cap of some kind, either a knitted one or one of those baseball caps. He had a little grey beard and he'd only ever been to a *tok ples* village school, one that was taught in the local language, not English. He loved reading.

Each day when I asked, "How should we start today?" Straightaway, they would point to the ABC chart. All of them loved reading and writing, especially cursive writing. I gave one fellow a book on cursive writing as a prize at the end of the year. He just loved it.

It was difficult getting help for the class. The only assistance we ever had was the money for supplies that came from the tiny parish of St John's Church, Crapaud, on Prince Edward Island, Canada. We also had donated offcuts of newsprint that we collected from the *Post Courier*, the national newspaper. These were of great value. From them, I made everyone's first writing book.

ONE DAY AT THE AIRPORT, I met a teacher with whom I had worked at Hagita. He asked, "Sister, what are you doing now? You're getting very old."

I said, "I'm teaching a literacy class."

He said, "I'm working with literacy now. I'm with the government in the Department for Literacy. Anything I can do for you, just let me know and I'll do it."

I said, "Good. I'd like some pencils and paper and some coloured pencils to draw with."

He said, "Oh, no. I can't give you that."

I asked, "What can you give me?"

He replied, "I can just support you by telling you to keep on going."

I bought colouring books and pencils but that didn't greatly interest the students. It was writing that was important to them, as was getting a mark for work they had finished. I used stickers of every kind on their books so getting a bird, flower or a coloured star meant a lot.

It was always a small group, 6 to 8 participants. Everyone was at a different level. With reading and writing it was all individualized. I checked their writing and listened to the reading but I needed help. Over the years several teaching Sisters who were retired came to listen to the reading. Sister Claire was the first one to come to my assistance. She offered to come over mid morning for the reading session. Sister Bridget followed and when she had to leave Sister Madeline took her place. This proved to be a great blessing as when I suddenly left Papua New Guinea, Sister Madeline took over the literacy class. Sister Therese Pe'eu joined her. To my delight they have kept the Tuesday and Thursday classes going.

THE LITERACY PROJECT allowed me to assist people that no one else cared about. My students were really doing what they wanted to do. There wasn't a great deal of preparation. I used the blackboard so I didn't have to print any worksheets. Whatever I put on the blackboard was what they wanted to write. Whatever book I opened was what they wanted to read. They had no great plans for jobs. I could give them what they really wanted. It was such joy being with people who didn't want anything except to learn how to read and write.

The women who came to my literacy classes had nothing. Eileen was the youngest of three daughters. The other two daughters went to high school, graduated and found good jobs. Eileen was the one who stayed home to do the housework. Her eldest sister came and said, "Sister, I want my sister to learn to speak English and to learn to read and write." Eileen was a most beautiful and gracious woman. She stayed with the literacy class for almost 2 years. Then she came and told me she was returning to her home province of Aitape, but at least she had learned how to read and write. She had something.

Most stayed for a year but Moses just kept turning up. Sometimes when I said something he would add on to it because we'd done it before so he knew what was coming. I'd ask something and Moses would give the answer because we had done it last year.

If I asked, "What will we do?"

He'd say, "Do this."

I'd say, "We did that last year."

He'd say, "We'll do it again." So we did. Every year I'd wonder if Moses would return and every year he would just turn up.

One woman asked if she could send two *wok bois*, young men who worked as labourers, to learn English. I told her they would have to come at the right time. She then asked me how much it would cost. I told her nothing. There was no fee. The two fellows were from the Highlands of Papua New Guinea and were enthusiastic students. They were great to have in a group.

FROM WHAT I COULD UNDERSTAND, the students in my literacy group all had *wantoks* with whom they lived. There's no government assistance for anyone in Papua New Guinea. Families look after their relatives but it gets harder as there might only be one or two people working with a wife and children to look after, along with parents, and other *wantoks*.

Wantoks are people from the same area who can speak that language. There are 770 different languages in Papua New Guinea. The *wantok* system was very supportive for years. For a long time anyone who was connected to you in any way was your *wantok* and you were obliged to help them. When paid employment came along, it became very difficult because *wantoks* would just show up and there were so many, it was impossible to help them all.

Now, people often live in towns with a limited wage which has to last for the whole fortnight. In the old days if Papua New Guineans wanted food, they just went out to the garden. If fish was wanted, someone would go fishing. If any kind of meat was wanted in the Highlands, someone went out into the bush with a bow and arrow. People had no need to store food. It took people a long time to learn how to live in a cash economy. As a result, the *wantok* system has become smaller. It extends to your immediate family but not to everyone else that claims a relationship with you.

Moses definitely had a home with *wantoks*. I would ask on a Tuesday morning, "What have you done since our last lesson?" I would begin by saying the sentence pattern,

"Since our last lesson, I have visited the Sisters at Marata. Since our last lesson, I have been to the store to buy some books. Since our last lesson, I have watched television and I have been to Mass."

I'd ask Moses, "What have you done since our last lesson?"

Moses would say "Since our last lesson, I have swept the house, I have worked in the garden and I have been to Mass on Sunday." So I knew he had a home.

The students were limited by what they could do and where they could go as they had no money. Often, conversation was challenging for me as I would have liked to talk about a film, a television show or a news story. Mind you, it didn't make them unhappy; it just made me sad. Moses seemed quite happy sweeping the house or working in the garden. Because he'd never had anything else, he didn't know that anything was missing from his life.

ANOTHER ENJOYABLE ACTIVITY for me at this time was our broadcast sessions with Radio Maria, the radio of the Catholic Church. Our radio sessions began in 2011 when, as Daughters of Our Lady of the Sacred Heart, we celebrated 125 years in Papua New Guinea.

I began writing a dialogue that told our story from the early days in France to the present. Sister Paula came with me as we made an hour's radio talk. The technicians were terrific. We made many mistakes but when it came on air we were perfect. When others heard the program they wanted to have a part. As a result, I would have a new co-host every month.

After preparing the script, choosing the music that was a suitable fit, my partner and I would practice the dialogue.

When ready, we would go to Radio Maria to record. Each session would be aired several times a week for the whole month. At the end of 2011 Radio Maria staff asked if there were other topics we could talk about. We did sessions on Liturgy, Gospel stories and the Pope's theme for the year, such as the Year of Mercy.

In 2014 the Catechism for the Catholic Church in Papua New Guinea and Solomon Islands was published. I had been part of the working committee that had produced this Catechism so was very familiar with its content. That became our next topic. It took over a month to cover each chapter. These sessions were welcomed by the laity and teachers. We regularly received positive and constructive comments from our parishioners and always a warm welcome when we arrived at Radio Maria. Maybe the most affirming comment came from our Sisters in Holland who rang to let us know they were listening to our Saturday morning sessions and encouraged us to continue. We did. With an enthusiastic co-host we had our monthly sessions until I left in September 2019. Re-runs of these radio sessions continue.

ANOTHER ENRICHING ACTIVITY was my involvement with Limana Vocational Community College. This centre teaches a variety of courses including tourism and hospitality, business and Grade 9 studies via Flexible Open and Distance Education for Grade 8 school leavers. Sister Maria Goretti, another of my first group of Postulants, began her vocational training at Sideia Vocational Training Centre and continued taking courses to improve her skills; she is the present manager. She has really worked wonders over the years in raising the standards of the Centre.

It was begun by one of our Sisters in the early seventies for girls who failed to be selected for high school after completing Grade 6. Now, it has added a limited number of male students to its intake. It has been raised to the status of one of the few National Community Colleges. I was a member of the Board of Management as well as several of the Board's committees including Staff Selection, Student Discipline and Agency Rights. Agency is the title given to any recognized education establishment that follows the National Education Syllabus and belongs to the National Unified System. I was invited for every wonderful celebration they had as well as their monthly School Mass and, during Lent, the fully acted Stations of the Cross.

Another idea originated in Canada when Sally Goddard asked me about the possibilities of developing a sewing machine project in Port Moresby. I talked to Sister Christine, an accomplished seamstress, who had at that time had just joined our community at Boroko. We agreed that the Settlement women, those without income living in shacks in the city, could be taught to make their own clothes.

Sally was able to talk about the project to several women's groups on Prince Edward Island, Canada. Women from St Peter's Anglican Cathedral, Charlottetown, and St John's Anglican Church, Crapaud, donated money for sewing machines. When they found out that the Goddards would be going to Papua New Guinea in the summer of 2013, material and sewing accessories were given by women across Prince Edward Island. The material available in Papua New Guinea is very limited. The material from Canada was "silks and satins and linen, buttons and bows." Every piece was treasured.

Sister Christine went shopping with the money and

bought four hand sewing machines, which is what the women use in the settlements and villages. She also bought one electric sewing machine to teach the finer points of sewing. The first lessons were held under the big leafy tree between the convent and the church. When the Parish Hall became available, she moved there.

When Sister Christine moved to an outstation, we joined forces with another congregation at the Diocesan Centre to continue the project. The Sisters sell some of the clothes made by the women and with the money made, they purchase more material. The women learn how to make clothes for their families and are able to make extra clothes which are sold at the markets.

In 2016, I travelled to Prince Edward Island, and once again, the women on the island donated sewing supplies. I ended the trip with five suitcases of sewing material to take back to Papua New Guinea. The people at Air Canada charged me $200 for 3 suitcases but they let the others on for free. In Sydney, when I checked-in to fly to Port Moresby with my 5 suitcases, I explained how kind everyone had been in Canada. The woman said, "We can do better than that." She didn't charge me anything. The fabric has all been used and the project continues. Sometimes, the simplest projects are the ones with the biggest impact.

All of the women greatly appreciated the material that came from PEI. Sister worked out a scheme that allowed the women to choose a piece to make a dress that could be worn at their graduation. As for the buttons that came, I had the first choice of medium sized buttons that I could use to finish off the crocheted hand towels that I was making.

. . .

ON SATURDAYS IN BOROKO, I had enjoyable involvement with three totally different groups of people. In the morning for an hour I took three young men who wished to improve their English so they could successfully move into an Institute of Higher Education. They wanted to attend the Catholic Theological Institute (CTI) at Bomana. It was a pleasure to see how they opened and improved as we worked together. In my final year I was taking a Korean Sister, who was living with us for a total immersion in English, several times a day for formal sessions. I invited her to join the Saturday morning group. It was amazing how much more life, energy and enthusiasm was generated when we had a small mixed group. At times I felt both were trying to show their English was better than the other. It led to improvement all round.

The parish priest invited me to take part in a Marriage Preparation Program. Each course lasted six weeks with a two hour session every Saturday afternoon. There were many groups, and each group was very diverse. This program continued for some years. One group had an Indonesian couple and a Buddhist man who was to marry a Catholic Indonesian woman. She was doing a similar course in Indonesia. He wanted to make sure he knew what she knew. I am not sure if the content of the two courses would have been the same. My content was church teaching and personal relationships.

One day a man asked, "Sister, how much can you know about personal relationships and family experiences if you have never been married?"

I replied, "I have watched three marriages very closely. My parents', my sister's and my niece's. Each one taught me what it takes to make a successful marriage. My mother's patience and understanding. My father's obvious need for forgiveness when he blew up like a volcano. My sister's love and devotion to her children when her husband was so often called away, and his appreciation of her willingness to put their family needs first. Finally my niece whose husband always put her first. On three weekends a year, Mother's Day, their wedding anniversary and her birthday, he took her away to an unknown destination. Even when their first daughter and then the twins were born he took her off. Their marriage always came first."

Each group seemed to enjoy the sessions and expressed their satisfaction at the end.

Later in the afternoon I would take a delightful Polish dentist for an English lesson. We became very good friends. Our sessions became an exchange of family tales. She had five beautiful children who had completed their primary school education in Papua New Guinea at St. Joseph International College and then returned to Poland to complete their education in various European Colleges.

In so many ways in so many fields I made truly wonderful friends in Papua New Guinea.

ELEVEN

TRAVELS

I HAVE BEEN fortunate to travel on occasion. Many of these trips have left lasting memories. My overseas travels began in 1975 with my studies at the EAPI, in the Philippines. They took off again in 1996 when I went to Issoudun, France for a Spirituality of the Heart workshop. Issoudun is where our Congregation was founded by Father Jules Chevallier. From Issoudun I went to Lourdes and then to Belgium and Holland where we had several old Sisters who had worked in Papua New Guinea. They greatly appreciated any visits from Sisters who came to Europe. In both countries, the Sisters took us around to see the main sights. From Holland we went through Switzerland to Rome.

The message that came to me in Rome was, 'This is what I believe'. I walked around the streets of Rome and no matter what I saw, I thought, 'This is what I believe'. We went to the Catacombs where there is a statue of St Cecilia, lying on the ground with one hand behind her back. That hand had the thumb and the first two fingers up. It is the sign that the Pope uses when he gives a blessing. It is the sign of the Trinity. St Cecilia lay on the ground dying for three days. She had a great gash across the back of her neck. Cecelia was saying, "This is what I believe. I believe in the Father, Son and Holy Spirit." It really was the most moving work of art.

We were told that an American whose wife had just died had come and seen the statue of St Cecelia. His wife was named Cecilia as well. He immediately had another statue made and taken to America for his home church. The story of St. Cecilia is that of a young woman who wouldn't give up her faith, who refused to marry a rich pagan man in Rome, so was condemned to death. She and others died for what they believed. 'This is what I believe'.

We went down underneath St Peter's Basilica and came to the place where St Peter's bones were. The guide shone the torch and shone the torch, still I couldn't see them. He kept shining the torch and asking me if I could see them. Eventually, I could see a tiny white spot so I said yes. 'This is what I believe'.

The cobblestones of the streets of Rome were laid in the time of the Roman Empire. I was walking on those stones that day. I know that the Church has much to answer for but it's not the faith that has to answer. The Church is what the people have formed through faith down through the ages.

I remember that beautiful movie, *Brother Sun, Sister Moon*, the story of St Francis of Assisi. St Francis went to the Pope in Rome to have his Congregation of Franciscans recognized as belonging to the Church. The Pope was sitting on a great high throne with an ornate mitre on his head. He looked like an overdressed king. St Francis had been given a script of what to say to the Pope. As he knelt before the Pope and opened the script, it fell from his hands to the floor. Then he said in his own words what he wanted to say.

The Pope came down from his glorious throne, bent down and kissed St Francis' feet. He said to St Francis, "You are what I was, not what I have become." Francis is who the Pope was as a young man. He had wanted to be like St Francis and set the world on fire. But things had taken him a different path into the world of politics and riches.

It is people who have formed the church and passed the faith down through the ages. That is the faith I saw in Rome. 'This is what I believe', I said as I walked around Rome. I went to Assisi where St Francis was born. All the time I said to myself, 'This is where Francis lived, this is where Francis worked and prayed. This is where the real faith lives'.

The Holy Land 2015

The sessions with the Postulants on the Old Testament prepared me for a very special time in my life. In 2015, I was able to spend time in the Holy Land where my knowledge of the Old Testament and the early life of Jesus was invaluable.

My visit to the Garden of Gethsemane was very special. We visited Gethsemane, just outside the city of Jerusalem. It was a very peaceful place, nestled on the Mount of Olives. It was where Jesus had prayed he would not have to suffer the horror that awaited him. Every Thursday, in our congregation, we make a Holy Hour. During that time I try to be with Jesus in the Garden.

When I was in the Garden of Gethsemane I lay down on the grass under an old olive tree to contemplate.

Everyone in the tour group thought I had collapsed. They were all looking out for me because I was so much older than the others in the group. They couldn't believe that I was 78. My time of quiet contemplation ended.

On another part of the journey, we were standing on the Golan Heights overlooking the Sea of Galilee. I could see the small area that Jesus would have covered in his lifetime. He dealt intensely with the people who lived there. The Sea of Galilee reminded me of the Milne Bay area. I could imagine how easily it could change. A strong wind could cause huge waves and make it difficult for the boats. From there we went down to the other side of the lake and went out into the Sea of Galilee. We sailed along the coastline of the area where Jesus would have lived among the people. I was walking in his footsteps.

The guide took us out into the desert and left us there to experience for ourselves what it was like to be in such a place. It was so hot, there was nowhere to hide. This desert was bare rocky hills. I kept thinking of the Jewish people journeying across this desert, looking for the Promised Land, and coming across one rocky mountain after another. Each time they reached the top of one, they had to go down and back up to the top of the next. There was nowhere to shelter. I now have a better idea of what that time in the desert must have been like for Jesus.

Overall, the trip gave me a deeper understanding of the places and geography in the Bible. It certainly gave me stories to share.

Japan

Japan made a deep impression on me. The morning after I arrived, I woke up to snow on the ground. I walked around in the snow enjoying the beauty of the many cherry blossom trees that grew on the grounds. I was totally lost in admiration until a priest came out and gently whispered, "When the Mother Superior is ready, everyone is waiting to begin Mass." I quickly hurried inside to join the others.

I couldn't be anywhere else except Japan. I saw the temples, the cherry blossoms, and all the signs written in Japanese. One cold wet day, we went out and had to travel by train. At the end of the platform where we were waiting, there was what looked like a statue of a woman. Her face was perfectly white with makeup and she wore a beautiful kimono. I stood there admiring her. Then, when the train came along the jolly woman moved! What I had thought to be a statue was a real woman.

Getting on a train was no problem. The guards just pushed and pushed until everyone was in. One weekend I was taken to visit Osaka. It was the time of the Cherry Blossom Festival. We saw beautiful traditional dancers in the city square and visited the national mint where famous ornamental cherry blossoms formed a canopy over all the walkways. We went for a drive from the east side to the west of the Island to visit places where the MSC Priests were working. As there was snow on the ground, we stopped so I could make my first snowballs.

Canada

My time on Prince Edward Island was wonderful. I had been invited there for a wedding. I tell people about it all the time. That first day, I didn't go to bed until 3 am and then was picked up at 9:00 am for a tour. We went to the Lieutenant Governor's and chatted with him and his wife as well as a Monsignor. Then, we were off.

I remember a potato chip factory, and I remember watching the potatoes grow because I drove past the same field so many times. We went to the cottage industry factory where you could take your pussy cat's hair or your dog's hair and have it made up into skeins of wool. I bought a couple of tea towels made by a woman working on her loom. I still have them. They are too precious to give away. Returning to Charlottetown, we saw the Amish in their wagons. That day, we were too late to see Anne of Green Gables's house but later someone took me to the house and to every single spot on which Anne might have stood. The Papua New Guinean Sisters loved the movie with Colleen Dewhurst as Marilla. Once they saw my pictures, it was difficult to tell them it was just a story.

On a Sunday morning, we had a huge breakfast down on the wharf at Victoria by the Sea, then went to St John's Anglican Church in Crapaud. It was one of the most beautiful masses I have ever been to. The celebrant was a woman priest which as Catholics we don't have. In the mass, there was a baptism of a baby. During the sermon, Rev Margaret talked about the three special events that were happening that day. The first was the baptism, the second was a priest who was celebrating 50 years of ordination, and the third was me, the first real missionary they'd ever had in St John's.

When she baptized the baby, she called the little brother who was about 4. She invited him to stand beside her for the baptism. She said, "You're going to be very important to this baby. You're going to help this baby grow. You're going to be his big brother. You're going to teach him, so you have to be here for his baptism." When they walked down the aisle to the front of the church, she asked the congregation if they would receive the baby into the congregation of Christ's flock. Everyone enthusiastically said, yes, they accepted the baby. Reverend Margaret was inspirational.

At the end of the service when she asked me to say something, I said, "This has been one of the most beautiful Eucharists I have ever celebrated." It was just lovely. That was a highpoint of my trip. Her husband, Eric, was a United Church minister. It just shows how when there is faith, religions can get on.

Travelling is so enriching for yourself as well as others. It helps you to see how people use their part of the world their way.

TWELVE
REFLECTIONS

On Language

CURRENTLY, the new education system in Papua New Guinea has primary schools teaching Prep to Grade 8. Prep 1 and Prep 2 are in the students' first language. They begin learning English as a subject in Grade 1. The children that I taught didn't know a word of English and I didn't know a word of their language. By the end of the year I could speak some of their language and they could speak English. They became beautiful English speakers as they grew up.

I went to a meeting and listened to a woman talk about teaching in the vernacular, the local language, for the first three years in school. She felt the students wouldn't understand anything for the rest of their lives if their local language wasn't used. After she'd finished, I stood up and said, "I'm very sorry but I can't agree with you because this is my experience." I told her of my teaching in English with the children talking in their language, and both of us learning from each other. I went on and said, "These students became the best in the province when they sat for the national exams in grade 6, in grade 8 and grade 10. They became teachers, nurses, whatever they wanted."

When I finished speaking, there was a great upshot of hands in the room. Many of the girls from the meeting were from Dogura which is the Anglican School in the Milne Bay area. They all said, "We agree with Sister. We learnt English. We never spoke our local language in school, we never learnt Pidgin. We spoke English all the time and now here we are in these positions. At home we always speak our own local language and even now we speak in the vernacular, so our children have not lost our language."

Children absorb what they hear. I think learning in the local language is important but I also think that learning in another language is equally as important. I remember a missionary family on Rossel Island who had a little boy. They sent him to the village school where the teaching language was Rossel Island language. This boy would come home and play with the children outside and he would talk using Rossel Island language. It was a language that few people could learn. The Missionaries who went to Rossel Island never learnt to speak the language, except for a few common words. Normally, wherever we went we learnt the local language but Rossel Island language was one language we could not learn. However, the little boy had no trouble learning it.

There are many dialects in Milne Bay. Every island has their own language and then different parts of an island will have a different dialect. On Fergusson Island there are 10 schools and each school has its own dialect. The people from different islands could understand each other. The people out East have Motu as a common language. The islands around Dobu, Normandy, Fergusson, Goodenough and the Trobs use Dobu as a common language. The older

Trobriand Islanders speak Dobu because of the interaction that takes place in the annual Kula trade. Most of the people could understand Dobu. On the Trobs, the people had two dialects, the coastal and the inland. No one has any difficulty understanding each other. We only spoke the coastal language but could always understand what everyone was saying.

Although there are over 700 different languages in Papua New Guinea, some of them are dying out. I was at a workshop for a few days. At night the women and I would have our meal around the kitchen table. Then we would just keep on talking. I remember one night I said to them, "Everybody say one sentence in your own local language." They all sat there, so again I asked them to say a big long phrase in their local dialect. The majority of the women there could not say one thing in their local language. They were losing their mother tongue. All they had was Pidgin and English.

In areas where Pidgin is being spoken it takes over from the local languages and it takes over from English. Pidgin is picked up very quickly and the people have learned it. It has become the language in the Highlands, along the north coast of Papua New Guinea, and even now it is becoming the language in Port Moresby.

I refused to learn Pidgin. There were people who came into government positions in Port Moresby from Pidgin speaking areas, and they brought Pidgin with them. Pidgin is one of the official languages of Papua New Guinea so people can use it wherever they like.

But because of this, English became less dominant. The managers of the banks in Port Moresby would contact the Headmaster at Hagita High School to recruit students into the bank from Grade 10. They knew the students could speak English. Students coming from other schools around the country were more fluent in Pidgin. I really think education has to be in English.

Pidgin is a language in its own right. It has a basic structure with its own grammar and its own rules. Pidgin is displacing the tribal languages of the people. There have been a number of attempts to discourage its use, but the language continues to grow in popularity. There are only about 1300 words in Pidgin. In comparison, the average English-speaking person has a vocabulary of 20,000 words.

In Milne Bay, where teachers are now coming from all parts of the country, they bring Pidgin as their language. When I was there in the late 90's, it was happening. On my visits to schools, we'd have a Mass or a prayer service and some people would want to sing Pidgin hymns.

I'd say, "No, we're not singing those. We're not singing those hymns. You sing hymns in English or in your own language, you don't sing hymns in Pidgin."

Someone would say, "Oh, but the teacher taught us!"

"I don't care who taught you. You're not singing them. This is an English speaking school so we will sing the hymns in English," I would reply.

That's why I never learnt Pidgin. I have a resistance to it. I gave a workshop for Sunday School teachers. I feel it was successful and everyone enjoyed it. At the end of it, one of the participants came to me, and said, "Sister, you'd be perfect if only you could speak Pidgin."

I said to him, "I'll never be perfect."

Now I feel I must say something about Pidgin from the point of those who live and work with this language. We had a priest in Milne Bay who in linguistic terms was a sponge. He just soaked up languages. After arriving at

Sideia in no time he was speaking to the people and preaching in their own language.

When he went to his first real appointment out east, where he worked for many years an old village man said of him, "If I close my eyes and listen to him I would say it is a man born in my village who is speaking." When I arrived in Daio it was he who gave me my first lessons in the language.

He followed me to the Trobs and helped me improve my language skills there. He loved the Island languages even though it meant learning a new language every time he moved. They connected him to the people. He had no time for introduced languages. Then he was asked to go north for a year, to Rabaul on the island of New Britain where Pidgin was the universal language. He returned completely converted, not to introducing it but to its value and its benefits.

By learning this one language, Pidgin, he could preach in any Church he went to. He could speak to people on the road, in the stores, at the market where people from miles around gathered, in the villages. People of every age and place spoke to and understood him. He found Pidgin to be very unifying. That is the experience of our Sisters who have lived and worked in this area. They love Pidgin. They value it. It is the common language of the wide, scattered area. This is true also of the Highlands as well as the mainland. Pidgin has its value. Pidgin has its place. It is recognized as one of the three official National Languages of PNG: English, Motu, Pidgin.

Here is an example of Our Father in Pidgin.
Papa bilong mipela, yu stap long heven.

On the Church

I think in countries in the Western world, religious life no longer has the attraction it once had for young people. I don't see that as totally negative. Today, lay people in the church are taking a greater role in all forms of the Apostolate, which includes health, education, administration, direction of charitable agencies, such as Caritus and other overseas organizations, as well as Retreats and Spiritual Direction.

When I was a child, there were no lay teachers. Religious Brothers and Sisters taught in schools. Now, in our Catholic schools, the laity has taken over. There might be one or two Sisters or Brothers in a Catholic school but the rest of the staff are lay people. These women and men do a fantastic job. They are beautiful with the girls in our OLSH colleges. They carry on the spirit we had. The Sisters instilled in us the love and compassion of the Heart of Jesus. Now the laity continue to pass on this spirit to the young women of today's world.

The teachers at Our Lady of the Sacred Heart College do much the same for the students as the Sisters did for me. Their students are young, compassionate — women of justice and peace, holding rallies and special days to raise funds for our international missions and environmental causes. They do great things.

I think there are great signs of hope. It's not a matter of crying or weeping over the past, but a time of rejoicing. It is in the emerging countries where Religious life is alive and well. We have just had seven young women enter with us in Papua New Guinea. In our worldwide congregation, Indonesia, a Muslim country, is our largest Province. The

Provinces of Papua New Guinea, Indonesia and South Africa are booming with promise.

Today, lay people are the voice of the church. Their role in the world as parents and professionals means they are deeply involved in all that is taking place and gives them the ability to speak on behalf of the rest of the wounded people of our world. I think it's a great thing that the laity are claiming their rightful place in the church and doing this successfully.

In Papua New Guinea, the Church is alive. The women in the Church in Papua New Guinea take an active role. Every Church, every parish has its Parish Council. They have their regular meetings. The community is really involved in the decision making of the parish. The priests in the parishes allow the laity to be involved in the running of the parish. The priests carry on the sacramental life of the church, but it is the people who organize the parish. They organize monthly visits to the jail to make sure prisoners are cared for. They take food, have prayer and singing sessions, and have all sorts of meetings with the inmates. It is the people who organize Religious Education for Catholic students in government schools. Lay chaplains regularly visit the main hospitals. Every week, laymen and women, Sisters and Brothers, give Religious lessons in government schools.

There have been tremendous changes in the Church since Vatican II with lay people recognizing their essential role.

———

On Papua New Guinean Independence

Independence Day 15th September 1975

One night a boy came to the convent to get a Band-Aid on his finger. There really was nothing wrong with it. I was doing the clinic that night as we didn't have a nurse and I told him that I was sorry but the clinic was closed for the night. I had better things to do that night than put a Band-Aid on a little sore. He said to me, "Sister, you just wait until we get independence and then you will put a Band-Aid on my finger."

I think people had strange ideas about Independence. The Papua New Guineans thought that all the expats would leave and they would have power. Our Provincial Superior sent a letter asking if we would give serious consideration to becoming Papua New Guinean citizens. We had young women who were with us as Papua New Guinean Sisters and they continued to need our support. We had discussions, we asked people in to talk to us, telling us whether it was a good idea or not. Finally, we decided that we wouldn't become citizens. We wouldn't be good citizens because of the colour of our skin. If people were going to have a fight and rebel they weren't going to walk up and ask if you were a citizen. Some of us decided not to become citizens.

The people in Milne Bay had no great desire for independence. They had been under the Australian administration for a long time and the majority were happy with that. The local Member of Parliament came to visit the students at Hagita to speak about independence. He was a member of Micheal Somare's party. One of the students said to him, "The people of Milne Bay would like to leave independence for one more year. If you have to vote on independence next week, what will you vote?" The member said he felt he would have to follow Michael Somare and vote for independence. The student replied, "Who put you into parliament, Michael Somare or the people of Milne Bay?"

There was a ceremony in Port Moresby with Prince Charles and the first Governor General, John Guise, who was from Dogura. He expressed his pride in the fact that when the Australian flag was lowered, it was not pulled down and burned. It was lowered with dignity, folded and given to Gough Whitlam, the then Prime Minister of Australia.

On the day itself, 15 September 1975, there were great celebrations in every city, town and village. The culture of every tribe and clan was displayed. The gratitude for the past and excitement for the future were filled and expressed in wonderful ways. Papua New Guineans can be very proud of how their country has progressed over years. Certainly, there have been many issues but there have never been any big problems between the different peoples in Papua New Guinea. There have been tribal fights between the people in the Highlands but these were a constant occurrence long before Independence. I think Papua New Guinea has been successful in what it has achieved since Independence.

POSTSCRIPT
SALLY GODDARD

I first met Sister Helen when she was teaching at Sacred Heart High School at Hagita in the 1970s. Later, when my husband and I transferred to the Trobs, she was there, wearing a white habit and going from school to school teaching religion, riding a motorcycle. Her openness and worldliness was a breath of fresh air to me, a non Catholic. Our oldest daughter was about 6 months old when we arrived on Kiriwina. Sr Helen would invite Nichola and I to the convent where they would chase geckos before she and I sat down for a cup of tea and a gossip.

After we returned to Canada, we stayed in touch first by letters and Christmas cards and more recently, using email. On several occasions when I returned to Papua New Guinea, Sister Helen helped with her many connections. She was able to come to Canada for our youngest daughter's wedding. At 80, her energy and delight in everything was infectious.

Initially, I was going to visit Australia in summer 2020 and spend time with Sister Helen recording her memories. Then COVID -19 happened and plans had to be adjusted. From the beginning of April 2020 until the end of July 2020, Sister Helen logged onto Zoom twice a week and chatted about her life. I ended up having to find people to help with the transcribing. Then, they stayed on to listen. All of us involved in this book have found ourselves marvelling at the way Sister Helen sees the world.

At our last Zoom meeting I asked Sister Helen for her 'life lessons', things that she had learned over the years that gave her the serenity she exudes. I would like to provide a summary in her own words.

Everyone has to believe in something
I learned what deep faith was from the people in Papua New Guinea. They believed long before we came. When the missionaries came and brought them the faith with Jesus, they really believed. Jesus is for them a person, God is a reality. You can't live life with nothing. You have to have some belief in your life. Their belief is God. God will get them through. They have a great belief in the afterlife. Everybody has their heaven. A person is not just here today and gone tomorrow. We're here today and then live for eternity. They have faith and a great trust in God.

Be optimistic
From my mother I learned to be optimistic. She sent me a card on my Feast Day once that said, "The will to help and the courage to do, a heart that can sing the whole day through, may the Giver of gifts give these to you." I've never forgotten it. I've used it over and over again in workshops. It doesn't matter

what happens as long as you keep on singing. The world's not going to fall apart.

Create meaningful relationships

My relationship with people has been from the heart. I loved the people in Papua New Guinea and I know I was loved in return. When Mum and Dad came to the Trobs, one of the women came to visit. She asked Sister Xavier, "Who is that woman?"

Sister Xavier explained that she was my mother. The woman then came and stood in front of my mother and talked and talked in the local language. When she finished, my mother turned and asked, "What did she say?"

I translated, "Thank you for giving her to us. Please don't worry about her. We will love her as you have loved her. We will care for her as you have cared for her. She will be our daughter."

That's what you were. I wasn't just another visitor. I belonged to the people of Daio and the Trobs as well as the teachers with whom I worked. Even the Highlanders would hug me and ask me how I was. I had relationships with the people.

A place is what you make it

My Uncle Fred told me that and I've remembered it. If you don't like a place, it will be no good. If you don't try to love the people that are there, you will be frustrated the whole time. Whatever circumstances you are in, they are what you make them. They'll be worse if you fight against them. Accept what you find and use them to turn into something positive. That way they will enrich your life, not drag you down. You don't have to have everything to be happy, you just have to work with what you have and who you are with. Don't aspire to be someone else. Just be yourself.

If you show fear then people realize you don't trust them

I always said the day I got scared I would come home. Out on the islands, the people protected us. I was scared on the boats but never of people. Even in Port Moresby I always felt safe. I was waiting for a PMV (a small bus) one day. When it arrived, there was no room. One scruffy looking fellow saw me wondering what to do and he told me to follow him onto the PMV. He pushed and pulled and made a walkway for me and actually got someone to give up their seat for me. Once I sat down, he climbed out the window and went on his way.

We have a choice. We can make things worse or we can make them better.

There is one last story from Sister Helen I would like to share.

One day I was in a supermarket in Australia, wearing my habit, and this woman came up to me and asked, "Sister, would you mind standing still and let my children look at you?"

I said, "No, of course not."

These children walked around me and touched my hands. They asked me if they could touch my veil. I agreed. Their mother explained that the night before they had watched The Sound of Music. *When they saw the nuns in the movie, they asked, "Who were they?"*

Their mother explained, "Those are the women who taught me when I went to school. We didn't have teachers like you do. We had these special women who taught us. We called them sisters or nuns."

Her children had never seen any nuns. She told them that there were still nuns but not that many.

When I walked into the store, it was almost like God had sent me on a mission.

I am convinced that Sister Helen's mission continues and lucky are those who have connected with her.

— *Sally Goddard, MSM*
  Charlottetown, PEI, Canada

APPENDIX: THE HOLY LAND

Thursday, May 28th, 2015

I AM HERE.

A Jewish taxi bus brought the eight of us to a magnificent edifice, Notre Dame, some form of Guest House and Study. There we changed to Arab taxies to come to our lesser accommodation in the Old City, which is in the Arab Quarter.

So breakfast, then I walked down to the corner for Trinity Sunday Mass. A beautiful little church that continues the excavated sight where Jesus met his mother on the way to Calvary. I went down under the ground to see it. The old man playing the organ played as if he was in St. Peter's so more than filled the little church. The mass was part English part Italian so I did not do too badly. Now to bed. I can miss lunch and come for the evening meal at 7.00. I am walking on air. My heart is singing. I am here in Jerusalem. Oh!

Friday, May 29, 2015

This morning I went off alone to follow the winding Via Dolorosa. "Just go straight," everyone said to me—who has no sense of direction. Fortunately everyone seems to have a suitable smattering of English.

The streets are amazing even though at 9.00 many of the street shops were not opened and so pleasant to move along. I asked a man sitting outside his stall if I were on the right road and he told me to go back and turn right, also selling me a map as guide. At the top of a steep street I asked again and was directed to the next left then left again. This brought me to the church of the Holy Sepulchre. A magnificent building which has steps going down many layers with excavations still continuing. I ventured down many levels then the legs said enough.

I bought a bottle of Coke to solve the liquid problem and was advised by a young shop owner I was drinking the wrong thing, his product it seems would have been better. I was enticed into many stalls but managed to just look except in the case of a beautiful blue cashmere shawl and an icon which I later realised I had paid far too much for. By now all the stalls were opened and the streets really crowded. Every stall owner could sell me something I needed but I kept straight ahead. Again the ground looked unfamiliar so asked and found I had passed the correct corner and had to retrace my steps. No great mistake really as the sights and sounds are amazing. I eventually came to a landmark in the church I went to on Sunday. I went in to rest before continuing up the final stretch to home.

I was in time for Mass in the underground church on which this building rests then lunch and a rest. I now feel ready for the official tour start at 17.30. I have changed all my times on the Programme to single numbers. Later in the Programme we move out first to Betlehem then Nazareth and the Desert. Looks very interesting. We are right next door to a mosque so get the regular calls to prayer. There seems to be singing and praying in the background from different directions at all hours. The lost luggage of my companions has been delivered.

Love and bye for now Helen

Tuesday, June 2, 2015

An amazing day. We spent the morning in the classroom being introduced to this strange, sad, surviving land. Lunch and then our first pilgrimage to Mount Scopus high above the City of Jerusalem. We walked down hill - remember what you walk down you have to walk up - to the Lion Gate which is the entrance to our part of the City. Then still on the downward slope to the bus stop. People, horns, buses by the dozen. Noise and life. Our bus finally came and took us up the steep hill to the top. We could see all of and around Jerusalem, out to the Dead Sea and beyond into the Desert. A clear day so a great view of past and present.

Back to the bus and half way down the hill to the Church of the Pater Noster. The prayer Our Father is written in hundreds of different languages on marble slabs around the wall surrounding the Church. At the back is an enclosed garden of silence and prayer. We had time to stroll around and then the call to move on, on foot further down the hill. It was extremely steep and a hand railing and my stick were both used as aids. Time for the evening meal so I will continue later. Bye Helen

Tuesday, June 2, 2015 continued

Now the day ends. I am not sure where the last email did. But I will continue from the church of the Our Father. We walked down the truly steep slope to the Garden of Gethsemane and came to an area where I could open a gate and lay down on the grass under an olive tree. This gospel story has become so precious to me over the years. It was a great feeling to lay there and feel and smell the grass.

From there to the Chapel of the Tears. We were told it is shaped like a tear drop but I could not get my head back far enough to see the truth of this. On the outside wall were vials meant as symbols to catch the tears maybe of those in this land, who have so many reasons to shed tears today. From just about every point the great golden dome of the central mosque, the Dome of the Rock, can be seen, it is the backdrop to the sheet of glass forming the front wall of this little chapel.

Now further down the steep incline to the Church of All Nations, so called as donations from almost all countries were used to build it. The Church of the Agony tells in striking mosaics the story of Jesus' night in that Garden. Now for home but how to get there? Down down to the bottom of the steep hill then up up the ever so stiff hill into the old city. Almost to the end and I had to sit on the stone seats set along the road no doubt for people like me. Two of the men, John, a nurse, and Adam, so kindly waited for me to catch my breath then carry on. In through the Lion's Gate continue up hill to the front door of Ecce Homo. I was ready for one place only.

It was truly a most wonderful day. Now our feet are standing within your Gates O Jerusalem. It helps to understand the joy the people must have on returning to this homeland. Now to prepare for tomorrow as again in the afternoon we become Pilgrims and travel to Ani Karin. Not the correct spelling but the home of Elizabeth and the birth of John the Baptist and the Magnificat. I shall surely be singing. My neighbour has just begun his call for prayer so I shall take it as a call for bed. My love Helen

NO DETAILS as we are just in from a day in the Judean Hills at Ani Karin where traditionally Mary went to visit Elizabeth. Again we climbed hills (mountains by my standards) and visited churches. But details tomorrow as we had classes till 12.15, lunch then left the house at 1.30 and we have just walked in after being dropped at a bus stop and it is 9.15. Bed surely calls. Love to all Helen

Thursday, June 4, 2015

Yesterday we went to Ain Karin, traditionally the village Mary went to to visit her cousin Elizabeth. We left by bus and circled through Jerusalem traffic through what is called the New City. Once out in the open we could move at greater speed — as it is only about 7 Km it was a short ride.

Out of the bus we walked to Mary's Well. Traditionally it was there for centuries where the village women met and worked now a rest hole for tourists and people like us. From there up yet another steep hill. Choose between stairs and flat stones with a hand railing. My age is being silently respected as two of the men seem to keep up with my step. I must say I am never the last to reach the stop. That may be because I keep my eye on the road until the summit and then look around at the magnificent Judean hills leading off into the desert.

After a rest on the step we went into the small chapel over which was built the main church of the Visitation. The small chapel tells of how Elizabeth hid her son John when Herod set out to kill all the boys under two years. I had never thought of John being connected to the event but as Ain Karin is mid way between Jerusalem and Bethlehem he was surely in the region. It is a lovely prayer spot.

Up dozens of stairs to Mary's place where the wall is covered with beautiful paintings of her involvement in the life of Jesus. The wedding feast of Cana with young girls as the serving maids. A new aspect of water into wine. A time for rest, silence and prayer then down the hill. The hand railing now not of much use as it was near boiling point with the afternoon sun. This is our first real taste of summer. Till now the days have been pleasant and the nights refreshingly cool to cold.

At the base we headed towards the church of John the Baptist which has a great painting of a really wild man of the desert. Next to the convent and guest house of the Sisters of Sion who conduct the Centre where we are based. A refreshing drink then free time. Many headed down the hill to the shops and ice creams while others, like me, settled for the surrounding gardens. Here I managed a picture of the Russian church. Its golden domes can be seen from every point of the City and surroundings but with trees and people it is difficult to get a good view. All returned for prayer in the chapel and then a delicious and much need meal.

Goodbyes, down yet another hill to the bus and home. We got off the bus to walk through the Damascus Gate which I was glad to do. Home and bed. Classes today and a free afternoon. There is an Irish Sister who knows the place so I will follow her. Tomorrow Bethlehem all day from 7.00 - 5.00 so see you when I recover. Love Helen

Thursday, June 4, 2015 (continued)

As we are going to Bethlehem for the day tomorrow and getting off to an early start I decided that with a free afternoon today I would rest. Then came the invitation from a Chinese Sister stationed here in Jerusalem to go sight seeing. It was terrific even though I covered much of the ground of the first day.

With no knowledge at all I had missed so much. I heard something of the Greeks, Coptics and Catholics all vying for space here in the Holy sites. I visited three churches of St. Helen and hopefully got some decent pictures as I seem to have finally mastered the camera. By the time we returned my feet were so sore. I soaked them for an age to get them reconstituted for tomorrow.

Friday, Jun 5, 2015

Today we made an early start for a full day in and around Bethlehem. With all in the bus with a packed lunch by 8.00 we were through the main street of Jerusalem before the work traffic came so we had a smooth, fast trip all the way.

As Bethlehem is only 8 miles from Jerusalem it didn't take long but a lot longer than it would to drive that distance in almost any other country. There was evidence of walls as soon as we left the Jerusalem area. It really is a most upsetting sight. Before entering Bethlehem we had to pass an

Israeli check point and for this reason we were told to take out passports and the special study three months study sticker we had received on entering the country. We needed neither as the bus driver called out the window "Americans!" And we were waved through.

We went first to the Catholic Christian University. This was established by and still conducted by the De La Sale Brothers. The Vice President is a Brother Peter from New Zealand. We were given a tour of the grounds and beautiful Chapel but had to pass by the library as it is being renovated. It has been damaged three times by bombing in the various wars. One bomb has been glassed in as a window as a reminder of the past. We went to the audio room to watch a short video of the growth of the Uni from 120 students to the current 4000 mixed Catholic, Christian, Muslim students.

Then four beautiful Palestinian students came to speak to us. Their story gives a totally new picture of life in this tortured land. They are truly prisoners in their own land. They cannot go outside the boundary without a permit from the Israeli Government. This could take months to be permitted or rejected for no given reason. Yet they keep hope that life will change.

As Br. Peter said, in the past 40 years great changes have taken place in South Africa, a wall fell in Germany, East Timor gained independence and Northern Ireland has peace.

There is hope for the situation here. A group of anonymous Israeli soldiers have started a group called Breaking the Silence. So many young people on both sides of the wall want to see real freedom for both nations and so there is hope. We promised our help in prayer.

From there back to the bus for a drive to the Field of the Shepherds and the Church of the Birth of Jesus. Nowhere near the actual site but so peaceful. We had a quiet time in the field followed by a talk by the co-leader of the course. In the church we sang some unseasonal Christmas hymns.

In the extensive grounds we had our picnic lunch before boarding the bus to visit a Franciscan Sister working with Palestinian families. Over the past ten years she has begun a reconstruction project to restore homes destroyed by the bombing, it is the destruction of homes and the growth in unemployment that has caused the greatest problem in families. Now the unemployed men take part in the reconstruction programme so are helping themselves in several ways. Sr. Maria had also opened a home for neglected or homeless boys from 6 - 16 until they go to uni or join her workforce. A most inspiring woman.

I forget to mention to get to her place we had to climb a hill you could not imagine. With a few stops along the way to catch my breath I managed very well. There were several willing arms offered when my knees weakened. I have never seen anything like the hills here. Those morning walks around the oval are sure paying off.

A short walk along comparatively straight streets to the Manger Square where we met up with our guide. He led us into the Church of the Manger with an explanation of the height of the three doors. The first really high by the first European builders. The smaller doors constructed by the Turks who destroyed most of the other churches in Jerusalem but left this one as they believed in the Virgin Birth but not the resurrection. Then an even smaller door that we had to stoop to enter put in by the Crusaders to put an end to anyone riding their horse into the church!!!

The main body of the church is undergoing repairs and excavation. A beautiful mosaic floor has just been unearthed and is in the process of being restored. We went down into the depths where we saw the silver star in the ground that marks what is supposed to be the spot where Jesus was born. Opposite is the place of the Manger. We each had a chance to kneel before or touch the spot. I got down knowing there were many helping hands if I needed it to get up but I managed on my own. From there we went into another cave under the church to the cave of St. Jerome who spent years translating the Bible from Greek into the common language of the day, Latin.

From here back above ground and across to the church of St. Catherine which is the actual Catholic Church in Bethlehem and where the Christmas midnight mass is celebrated. Now a correction—it was under this church that we visited the cave where Jerome lived and died.

The official day over we were free to shop. We were directed to a special store where we were assured prices were reasonable. It was so lacking and prices not so agreeable to me I left and went further down the street where I shopped and was given discount for coming. By now my feet were complaining so I found a cement block and settled to wait. It was 5.00 before we were in the bus and heading for Jerusalem. Now bed. Thanks to anyone who has written please take this as the reply. Blessings to all. I am having a marvellous time and standing up well at the end of the first week. Helen

Sunday, June 7, 2015

Today began in the classroom with a session on Luke's

gospel. At 3.00 in the afternoon a Father came to talk. This was Doctor Paul, a White Father - a name given to this group when they first went to Africa wearing their long white robes. This a name that now follows them across the world. He is a renowned teacher and writer of the excavations done on sacred sites in Jerusalem. The Church of the Holy Sepulchre is his speciality. For an hour he gave an amazing account of the building, destruction, re-building, so many times of the Church it seems it has now been established that this is the authentic site of the death, burial and Resurrection of Jesus.

We walked the street that covers the Way of the Cross and made our way, this time to a back entrance of the Church. I found the previous visit with Miriam and Agnes had covered most of the main areas. It was Calvary I had missed. That was the first chapel Fr. Paul took us to. I had seen it before without realizing its significance.

It really is impossible to pray or be silent as there are people coming and going by the dozen all the time. We were told that in the early hours of both morning and night many Muslim women come here to pray before a beautiful image of the Sorrowful Mother. This shrine separates the Catholic and Orthodox chapels on Calvary. The historian could offer many points of interest about the building of columns and the meaning of designs as we moved through the different sections. Still I have not been into the actual tomb as the queues were unending at both times. Like the Muslims it will have to be an early morning or evening visit for me to get that.

At the end of the explanation we each went our own ways. One of the women, Annette, and I walked back together for a while until Adam joined us. She then went off home and Adam became my guide. We were stopped at one stage by a large group of South Americans making the Way of the Cross. The streets are narrow and on Saturdays the stores spill out onto the streets. Add to that a procession of pilgrims there is nothing to do but to stand still.

We were home in time for the final session of the day which was a short evaluation of the week. How could you sum up in a few words all it has meant? Tomorrow an official visit to the Citadel of David at 11.00 then the day is free. It is suggested we visit the Israeli Museum and I have purchased a public transport ticket for that. A bit like an Opal card so I hope it works as effectively. I have knowledgeable companions as guides. Love now Helen

Sunday, June 7, 2015 continued

I am home early. There is just so much my feet can take on these rough stone pavements. Only in this house do I find a stretch of really flat floor. After 9.00 Mass we set out as a group at 10.30 for the Citadel of David. It seems most places we visit are via the Via Dolorosa and pass the Church of the Sacred Sepulcher. I could not get lost in that area now.

We are living in the Muslim Quarter of the city. There are the Christian, Jewish, Muslim and Arab sections. I have yet to work them out. While it is safe for us and tourists to walk in any Quarter it is not so for those who live here. If a taxi is needed when we go out it is an Arab or Muslim taxi we must call for. If we get any other kind they will drop us at the Gate. That means at one of the four Gates in the ancient wall that surrounds this section. Although this is the Muslim Quarter the Israeli soldiers are free to walk about and they do, making their presence obvious. A complex situation.

So we set out and finally came out at the Jaffa Gate and I found we had only to cross the road and the citadel was in front of us. To walk in the citadel a delight, the air so cool. Each person was given an audio device and direction to go. I shall not go into detail but it was an amazing experience. The whole history of Jerusalem as I have learnt it from Ancient History, the Bible and my own teaching over the years. I keep finding myself saying, "Oh if only the young ones were here with me! How well you would understand the Background of Jesus!"

I walked at my own pace, stayed as long as I wanted in each room or section. Once outside I was looking at the City as it has grown over thousands of years. Herod's Palace is still there. The walks built by so many different conquerors, the walls destroyed by so many invaders. It was fantastic.

Up and then of course down, ancient stone stairways all complicated as I tried to hold a camera, walking stick, listening device and handrail. Everyone is in admiration of the fact I am managing to keep up. No problem those daily walks around the cricket oval and down to the bus stop and up to the convent are now standing me in good stead.

But my feet on those rough stone streets! Still a soaking in hot water and then add Vaseline an Irish Sister has advised me and it seems to be doing the trick. After the Citadel many went on to the Israeli Museum but for me enough. What I have seen was well worth while and so beautifully done. The actual places, models diagrams - all that is needed to give a clear image was there.

This week we go to the desert on Tuesday and return Thursday evening so something to look forward to. Love now Helen

Monday, June 8, 2015

Today the place is silent. I seem to have it to myself. On Sunday we had a social gathering to celebrate the successful ending of our first week. It was very pleasant. Everyone brought something from nuts, grapes, drinks, home made sweets - from the local souk stalls - and a variety of others. Damien one of the teachers in the group from Sale brought his guitar and showed his real talent. Chris and Mark the two coordinators of the Programme added their talents and music filled the air. I left at 9.30 as I knew we were to rise early for the visit to the Golden Dome so important to Jews, Muslims and Christians.

By morning I knew I needed a day of rest. I got up and prepared a picnic lunch and had breakfast with the others then excusing myself went back to bed. I slept for three hours and woke feeling better and ready for tomorrow's early departure for our two days in the desert experience.

From the Programme this looks to be a quiet time with the only real activity a float in the Dead Sea. I am sure I will get a visual and oral description of today's outing. Several in the group are excellent photographers. So to continue my programme for the day I shall give myself the rest I need to keep going. The last few days have been fairly hectic. See you after the desert as I am sure the iPad will be of no use there.

Tuesday, June 9, 2015

Today I swam or floated on the Dead Sea! An amazing experience. I was like a cork bobbing on my back and then no way could I get up. I just rolled over and of course all the things we were told not to do just happened. Worst of all I got water in my eyes. I was like a blind person floundering. Thankfully two of the women in the Sale group, Angela and Jen, were most attentive and came to my aid. They turned me right side up, led me to the beach and handed me to Bernadette and Trudy, members of the staff, who took me to the public shower where I washed my eyes and like the blind man I could see.

Now of course that is beginning in the middle so I shall now go back to the beginning. We each packed a lunch, had breakfast and walked out the front door at 7.00. Once again downhill and out the Lion's Gate where the bus was waiting. Unfortunately as we drove out of Jerusalem around extremely narrow corners the driver clipped something on a hand railing. That took a short while and then off again.

Our first stop was at the Monastery of St. George, mid way between Jerusalem and Jericho so the Good Samaritan came to mind. The monastery was one of those built in the side of a cliff. How can they get in and out? In these days they say they have a small van. Their water flows under the ground through the hills - remember there are hills everywhere - from Jerusalem. They also had lots of solar panels in view. All around are dry dry hills.

All the time I have been here the line running through my mind is "like a dry weary land without water." On one of the hills we saw a shepherd with his small group of goats. Then as we turned round to walk back to the bus across the hills came four fellows on donkeys. This land is surely ageless.

Again into the bus and on our way to Quram where the Dead Sea Scrolls had been found. The wind from the desert was so hot. We found a shady spot under shelter while our knowledgeable guide, Jarard, gave the story of the scrolls and also of the excavated establishment we were about to visit. Jarard is an American born Jew. When he finished school, he went to Boston uni where he met so many Jews he decided he had to learn more about his homeland. He came and never left. He is now married here with a family.

From a distance we looked and saw the cave where the scrolls were found. His story was a small shepherd boy trying to bring back his wandering flock threw a stone that went into the cave. It hit something that made such a strange noise he went up the hill and into the cave to investigate. Hence the finding of such a treasure. We then walked through the excavations that people are working out to whom they belong. A community of men like the Ascenes or a group that made pottery. It is amazing that the walls of rooms used over 2000 years ago are still standing. The great thing about the walking was it was all flat. No stairs!

Again time for the bus and soon the water of the Dead Sea came into view and we followed it for the rest of the way. I was totally amazed at the size of the Sea. 70 Km long. The guide said it was formed at some great earth change when the mountains split forming the Judean hills and the Hills of Jordan. There is the north and south sea with the north a very rich blue and because of the salt the south is a pale green. Of course when you get in to float it is just colourless water. Still an amazing experience as I told you at the beginning.

So now the last part of the bus trip through the desert. It was so colourless really. Sometimes black rock and cliffs then it becomes a lighter brown, then a sandy brown, next grey and finally white. No vegetation for miles just stones, rocks, cliffs. Great chasms, high mountains and sharp cliffs. I could not take my eyes off the passing scene. If John the Baptist had stepped out onto the road I think I would not have been surprised.

The further south and lower we went small shrubs and bushes began to appear. Just like the hills dull, no real colour. We came into a few Jewish kibbutzs in the middle of the desert, even bus stops began to appear along the road. Shocking in a way with no real life anywhere else in sight. At last we drove into the kibbutz where we are now spending the night.

They say there is a beautiful big swimming pool here and most of the group made use of it as soon as we arrived. I went to sleep for a while. Now after a delicious meal in a beautiful dining room we are all gathered around on a verandah. Now we are beginning to move to rooms and bed so goodnight. We have an early start tomorrow to lunch with a Bedouin community. No time for corrections. I hope it makes sense. Just know it's amazing, wonderful, inspirational. Love Helen

Wednesday, June 10, 2015

I am sitting out in the desert. The air is crisp and cool around me, the sky almost black as the sand storms of Egypt and Jordan come across. The cocks are having a fantastic battle as to who can get the loudest and longest cry. Small sparrows are hopping around looking for left over crumbs.

Small date palms are planted around, for show I think, not dates. Yesterday we passed many date groves with trees laden with fruit ready for harvest in a week or two. I am told we are sitting on the Egyptian and Jordanian borders. In the kibbutz I stayed in a three bedroom in an L shaped building with four other double rooms. Many of us were disappointed we were not sleeping in tents. Would have been nice to wake with a camel's head poking in the door opening.

The road system is amazing. Not a bump all the way. A highway through the desert. We did come to one detour as we drove along the coast of the Dead Sea: a sink hole had opened up so a new road created. Because the Dead Sea has been so reduced by "development" the exposed land once dried out by the sun becomes a layer of crystals that just give way under any pressure. They have life savers on the beach not for sharks but sink holes. Stay within the flags.

Going back another crop we saw was cacti grown for aromatic reasons. Now I have to go. Hope this makes sense as the light is not good for an iPad and I shall not correct it. Love Helen

Wednesday, June 10, 2015

An early breakfast at the kibbutz and then on the way. I had risen early and sat out in the cool mountain air. It was so still and quiet until the rival gangs of local roosters began their competition. They reached notes I had never heard. Then a new sound that I did not recognise but was later told it was peacocks calling. What a shame I did not see them.

Yesterday as we drove into the Dead Sea town we entered a National Park. Our guide told us there were many ibex there but they only came out in the cool of the evening. Just then a mother and her babe came out of the bush. They looked like miniature deer, fragile and graceful. The next thing was Crown Casino Dead Sea. Does the Packer Empire reach this far?

Back to today. After breakfast an early start as we

headed for a prayer point. At a bend in the well sealed road our bus turned off the well beaten track which was rough going up and frightening coming down. At the top of a steep ascent we got out and walked to a flat area where we could sit on stones. No form of shade. The scenery was amazing.

We were on a cliff and down below stretching away to a range of mountains was rough uneven ground. At times there were miniature mountains pushed up. It looked like creation at the beginning of time before grass or plants appeared on the earth. Behind the row of mountains we could see the peaks of another range. It made me think of those people coming out of Egypt. Climbing those rough unfriendly mountains and expecting to find a land flowing with milk and honey in front of them. Only to find a wide area of rough land and then another range of mountains.

This is a land of mountains, wild rough unfriendly. Don't imagine Jesus in a flat sandy desert. He was in a place like this. All the way from Egypt to Jerusalem are mountainous plains, hostile to people and animals. The poor sheep and goats do have such rough land to cover to get a feed. Our guide led us in a meditation then we had 20 minutes alone. I found enough shade to protect one arm that had been getting more of the sun than the other during our guides fantastic explanation of this land and its history.

Back on the bus and the fearful descent until we were back on the sealed road.

We were on our way to a Bedouin's place for lunch. This is one group of people sadly affected by the formation of the Jewish State. They are one of the earliest groups to settle this land and have always been nomads. That does not suit the modern political situation so the government has provided land for these people to settle in.

A small number of Bedouin have moved into a small

town called Bel Shevha. This town has developed little since its beginning. Opposite is a large city Be'el Sheva, a Jewish settlement that has flourished and now has the Ben Gurion university and a large hospital. Between the two is the suburb of Omar where the professional people of the city live in high class modern homes.

The majority of Bedouin tribes have refused to move into the appointed area as that means to give up much of their ancient beautiful culture. All this we learnt from a conversation between our Jewish guide and Bedouin host. A delicious meal was provided for the 40 of us and then the women displayed the crafts they do to sell. Of course we all admired and purchased something.

It would have been good to talk more. Many Jews are sympathetic to the situation and hopefully these people will not have to abandon their lands and life style. The tribes who refuse to move to the settlements have no water, electricity, school or clinics in their areas. If they build on their land they receive a notice giving them 72 hours to remove the building or have it demolished. Better to take it down yourself than to have the destruction and show of force the government sends in.

We moved on to Abraham's Well. We looked up Genesis chapter 23 and read the story as we found ourselves sitting in front of that exact well. What - 2500 years later! We then walked around the excavated remains of a Jewish fortified town. Family homes, government buildings and the town gates. The brave then walked down dozens of steps into the depth of the earth to follow the path of the village's underground water system. The faint hearted with me among them walked on firm ground back to the bus.

Where to now? Home to Jerusalem. Slowly the desert

scene changes and vineyards, fields of sunflowers, market gardens and fruit trees begin to appear. We pass through check points to get into the West Bank of the Palestinians then back into Israeli area. So impossible to fathom.

Now home with tomorrow to prepare. More tunnels and then the four Quarters of the Old City. I must get to bed. It is wonderful, marvellous, amazing and I am enjoying it all. The group is so good to me carrying excess luggage and helping me along. God bless and love Helen.

Thursday, June 11, 2015

This is just an early morning report. This morning we got off to an early start at 7.00 and have just returned at 9.00 from walking underground the full length of the Western or Wailing Wall.

We were actually down to real Roman roads. The exact roads leading into the city gates to the Temple Entrance. We even stood at the back wall of what was the Holy of Holies in the old Jewish Temple.

A small room was full of both Jewish and Muslim woman praying at the back of the Holies of Holies. Who would ever have thought I could manage to get down so far? It is truly awesome. We saw and touched the actual bricks designed by Herod the Great to build the Temple after the destruction of Solomon's Temple.

The wall of great height is still standing. We walked the full length. We saw the efforts made by the Romans to destroy it and then they gave up as the foundations were just so enormous. We had to walk through the still unopened markets to the Wall but then came out from under the ground almost at our front door. What relief we didn't have to walk home. Our guide is truly knowledgeable. He answers questions without hesitation. He now takes us for a class then this afternoon we visit the Four Quarters of the Old City if I last the distance. It is all all all walking. Love now Helen

Thursday, June 11, 2015 (later)

What I sent earlier was a brief account of our morning walk —replacing my walk around the oval. At last, with the assistance of one of the women I seem to have captured the way of using the iPad properly for photos so hopefully I have some good shots. It is so amazing what I am seeing and learning from our wonderful guide. He moves so easily between each culture. Arab, Bedouin, and Jewish communities. Everyone who passes has a short word with him.

To get to the Western Wall we had to pass through a security check. It is amazing how many sensitive places there are and the Western Wall is definitely one of the most sensitive. Before the 1967 war a Muslim township was built right up close to the Western Wall and left only a narrow passage for Jews to walk along to get to the wall, which was the only remaining closeness to the old Temple. As soon as the Jews gained control of the Old City they bulldozed this township. The tension caused by this still remains. I am giving you some of the history from our Guide.

So down underground. We were given a fantastic demonstration with a model building of how Herod built the third Temple on the highest point in Jerusalem. Incredible what was done in a time with only human and animal muscle. Herod wanted a pattern created around each of the huge stones forming the basis of the Temple. We saw those stones forming the basis of today's Western Wall. We gasped at the size of each stone. No wonder the Romans gave up the effort to destroy the Temple. Hard as it was to build it harder still to destroy it. So they got it down to ground level but left the foundations which remain today for us and as the foundation for part of modern Jerusalem.

As our guide stopped at important points to give an explanation women, Jewish and Muslim, passed through, round the group. At last I asked what for. Was this a sort cut to the market or prayer areas? No they were coming and going to pray at the real wall that was the outside wall of the old Holy of Holies in the old temple. We stopped stood before and touched the real Wall of the Holy of Holies. Can you believe that? We were really back at a wall in a place 2100 years old.

Our tunnel became narrower and we had to walk single file until we came to a wider area and we found we were overlooking a great body of fresh water. This is a cistern built in Herod's times to provide water for the Temple cleansing ceremonies. Amazing!

Now to lunch and our afternoon understanding of the Four Quarters. Jewish. Muslim. Christian. I am off love Helen

Thursday, June 11, 2015 (continued)

Now to continue my day. I had a quick lunch as I wanted to get on the bed before the afternoon session of a walk to each of the four Quarters of the Old City. It is really too difficult to explain the complicated situation of Old and New so I shall leave that for my return for anyone interested. So the Old City inside the wall built hundreds of years ago is just one square kilometre in size with 400,000 permanent residents, so it is the most densely populated area in the world. It is divided into the Muslim Quarter, the Christian, Armenian and Jewish Quarters.

While not having the largest Quarter the Muslim is the largest in number having, and still growing, 36 percent of the population. Most residents are recognised as permanent residents but they refuse to take Jewish citizenship.

We are in the Muslim Quarter as are a remarkable number of Catholic establishments. There are at least three huge Catholic residences in this street. All connected with the first three Stations of the Cross. There are church spires poking up all over this part of Jerusalem.

Right next door we have the local mosque so five times a day, including 4.00 am, we hear the call to prayer. At 6.00 and 12.00 day and evening church bells toll and sound fantastic. So we are off through the Palestinian souk, market, up into the residential area where graffiti covers the wall. This is a sign of someone has been away and returned home.

From there we went to the Christian Quarter which includes all denominations. Their population is slowly decreasing as it becomes more and more difficult for them to thrive in this situation. It is the same in Bethlehem. Signs over the door indicate the nature of the community. Here we saw the first signs of European architecture left by the French and English. Next, to the Armenian Quarter which is a walled community within a walled City. This community moved here after the Turkish genocide around the time of the end of the World War. As the British drove the Turks out of Jerusalem the Armenians moved in. There was none of the colourful market stall here as had been in the other two Quarters.

Now the last of the Quarters, the Jewish Quarter here a

great change. This is a well planned suburban area only built after the bombing of the 1967 war after which the Israelis took over the whole City of Jerusalem. Here there were orderly houses and homes, none of the cramped conditions as in the previous Quarters.

Here we departed for the last time with our truly remarkable Guide, both so knowledgeable, clear in explanation and so affable. We walked home through the Jewish markets. Again such noticeable differences. Larger, tidier and more expensive goods. Quality art displays and beautiful clothes. Home and a rest before the evening meal. I was pleased to be able to make a Holy Hour at 6.00 in union with those honouring the feast of the Sacred Heart. Happy Feast day to all.

To end the day we went to see the Sand Picture artist. There are light celebrations every night for ten days. They end on Sunday night when we go to a Sound and Light show at Herod's Palace where we were sight seeing last ? Sunday. We saw then the beginning of the preparations. The sand artist lady tonight was amazing. For 15 minutes she created beautiful pictures just with a handful of sand. That was enough. All of the small group were ready to come home. I had an assistant every time we came to a step or a steep slopping road which was most of the time. The group is most attentive of me. Bye now. My love Helen

Friday, June 12, 2015

I have lost count of the days. In the chapel this evening I had to ask a lovely young Irish volunteer here if it was Friday or Saturday. The days are going by in such a whirl and with so much activity. It was a relief and pleasure to have sessions today in the classroom.

We began the day with the Mass of the feast of the Sacred Heart celebrated in the lower cathedral here. The celebrating priest really makes it a celebration. We all prayed especially for the MSCs and their works and in spirit I was at Kensington for everything. All here wished me a happy feast day as it was our main feast so I accepted all the blessings.

The church here is called a Basilica as it is supposed to have the paving stone Pilate stood on when he presented Jesus to the crowd and said, "Behold the Man." And so the name for the building is Ecce Homo. The church right next door commemorates the scourging of the pillar. It is the second and third Station in the Way of the Cross. I think I told you the street we are in is the Via Dolorosa. I cannot get lost even with my dreadful sense of direction as every one in the Old City can direct me to this street which stretches from where we are to the hill of Calvary and the Church of the Holy Sepulcher.

After morning class with a free afternoon I had a good rest then walked to the Wailing Wall as I missed out on seeing it on the official day as that was the day I took off. I also needed to get some cash but no matter how I tried the machine would not work.

Before going up to the Wall I washed my hands three times at a well as I saw others doing. There were taps rather than buckets for the water and "golden" ewers to collect the water and pout it over your hands. Then I walked up to the wall and, with the other women, stood with my forehead resting against the Wall. It is surely a very sacred place. Every one shows such great reverence and respect. I prayed for each one and all.

I enjoyed walking slowly along by myself looking and listening to a strange language. At the corner at the bottom of our hill I called into the church that marks Jesus meeting his mother. It is a beautiful place for prayer with signs for silence and no photos so all is still.

Tonight a small group walked 40 minutes there and back to a Hebrew Catholic Mass. As it was all walking I decided to wait. We go there one evening this week for the Eucharist and a lecture from the Sr who is in charge at that Centre. As we shall again be walking I shall have to get off to an early start. So ends another day. Love to all Helen

Saturday, June 13, 2015

We have just returned from the Night Spectacular at the Citadel of David. Every one has a different word for it. If I used them all I could not explain what it was like. A magnificent feast in sound and light of the history of Jerusalem. Amazing. Certainly indescribable from here. Maybe when I get to see you I shall be able to give you some idea of what we have just witnessed. It ended with Pray for the Peace of Jerusalem. Something that is sorely needed. Good morning for you now as I head off to bed. Love Helen

Sunday, June 14, 2015

I am just home from the Israeli Museum and while I found it in the most part like every other museum it certainly had the added attraction of the Dead Sea Scrolls. It was wonderful to see them after being in the very place where they were found when we were having our Desert experience last week.

Also our very informative Guide at that time mentioned the Ellepa Codex which at the time made little sense but today I saw what he was talking about. While in the Christian tradition we have several different translations of the Bible, like the Jerusalem Bible, the Good News Bible, the NRSA version the Jews have just one translation. Every printing has to be made exactly the same, word for word as that. I saw the Ellepa Codex, named after the town in Turkey where for so many years it was preserved. These documents go back thousands of years.

I also saw an old altar of sacrifice with a stone shaped like horns on each corner. If some one was in trouble and held onto one of these horns they could not be touched. They were places of sanctuary before temples or churches were built. Then outside I saw the stone doorways of former synagogues. All that is very enriching for the sessions I do with our novices in PNG. Now I will really know what I am talking about.

The other good thing about this morning was that I did not walk all the way. I travelled by both light rail and bus. Both dry modern, comfortable and fast on such heavily trafficked narrow roads. I had decided to go nowhere today but at breakfast one of the men Donald, the only Western Australian in the group, asked me if I would like to go to the museum as I had pulled out last Sunday after walking around David's citadel. He had done the same. I agreed to go knowing it would be almost impossible for me to find my way there by myself.

It came to me last night after we had wound our way through what really seem dark alley ways when all the souk is shut down, what it would be like for young parents to be looking for a twelve year old lost boy in such a place. Then it would have been Roman soldiers at unexpected corners. Now it is Israeli soldiers you meet. They don't do anything but they are a presence.

I travelled home with two young women in the bus and

noticed the handcuffs, radio and revolver hanging on her belt. But all is quiet for us. It seems it may be graduation time for them at the moment as there was a huge crowd of them visiting the museum as we were. Lovely young people ready to help even without being asked. When Donald just said out loud "Now where do we go from here?" one beside us gave directions to the light rail station.

Tonight we have early meal at 6.00 then I think it is a visit to a Catholic Jewish community led by a Jesuit from some European country. That might be tomorrow night. I do not have the programme with me at the moment. After my morning out I am sitting on the floor in my room eating my cut lunch. We had a life saving cold coffee at the end of the visit but as there was nowhere to sit we brought our lunch home.

We have had fantastic weather for this time of the year. The nights are cool enough for the light cover on the bed and the days moderate. It was hot walking back at 2.00 this afternoon. Did I tell you I was wrapped in the white jacket Sue got for me and a shawl at the Light and Sound show last night? The wind was strong and cold and cold. Now to rest. I pray you are all well. When I was visiting Mart's tomb yesterday I wrote in the book and even put one name for good measure. All my love to each. Thank you for your interest. Helen

Saturday, June 20, 2015

Well from the Hebrew Catholic Community to a Jewish synagogue for Shabbat Prayers. Today has been a free morning. So after Mass at St. Ann which began at 6.45 and ended at 7.45 I hurried home for breakfast. Streams of

Muslims on the road all heading for the Golden Dome or the Dome of the Rock as they call it. Then followed a stream of soldiers. It really must be both intimidating and shameful for the Muslims to have such a might imposed on their festivities.

Here there are great festivities and a lot of noise especially once the daily fast ends. The prayer call is louder and longer at the specific hours and I am happy I sleep through them all. Drums beat any time of the night. A canon blasts to mark the beginning and end of the daily fast. All the streets in our Quarter are lit up and it looks beautiful from our third floor terrace. After tea tonight we all moved up there for an evening talk and music. The usual second floor had been taken over by a group of 40 French people who came a month earlier than they had booked. People scampered to make beds and prepare them a meal.

At 4.00 we gathered to go by bus to the synagogue. The bus comes to a road outside the Lion Gate and I can tell you it is some walk past the Gate. On the return we are dropped at the Damascus Gate at the other side of the Wall. I prefer that as there is no hill to climb except for the last stretch. We of course have to walk down the many steps as we walk through the market place which is always a squeeze. But pleasant smells of food cooking, fresh bread, spices and fruit. Colour with the sights (oh the lolly shop. You would not believe what tempting sweets they have displayed on the street stalls). Then the people in their droves. When I turn the final corner at the fourth Station, a beautiful little church, the hill begins. Ecce Homo is it appears dead centre in the one long street. It is on the peak of the hill so going or coming there is always a hill to climb.

So by bus to the synagogue where we were given an

Introduction into the Saturday evening Shabbat prayers. Unlike us they still have to turn up for the Saturday morning Service. We had the English translation of all that was said. The continuous chanting throughout was very calming and soothing. You are permitted to sit through all of the prayers or stand and often bow or sway at certain times. There was no reading which I found disappointing.

    The service was led by a woman Rabbi as it was a moderate or Liberal Synagogue. Both men and women are allowed to wear the little skull caps. It lasted a full hour. Our bus was waiting when we came out as the driver, a Muslim, had not yet broken his fast so was keen to get home. I was keen for the same reason. By that time it was 8.00 as we sat down at the table. Bye for now. May all have an enjoyable weekend. Blessings from the truly wonderful Holy Land and love Helen

Sunday, June 21, 2015

As I begin this I am on a bus on my way to Galilee. The bus is swerving and so my finger hitting more incorrect keys than usual. I shall have to correct tonight if my eyes allow me. Last night was my first to be disturbed by the Ramadan activities. I heard the drum beating at regular intervals, the canons firing so loudly I wondered if anything more sinister was happening, then of course the untimely calls to prayer. Maybe it was the fact I was conscious of our early rising and departure. Now for a PS I have since heard a Muslim youth attacked an Israeli soldier with a knife. The Muslim is dead and the soldier fighting for his life. So certainly more than the canon.

    Back to Saturday when we had a weekly review session in the morning and then a free day until 4.00 in the afternoon. I rested for the day I had on Friday as I knew I was reaching the end of my reserves. That afternoon we had a fantastic explanation of the differences and situation of the Eastern Churches and Latin or Roman Catholic Church in Jerusalem.

I could never claim to understand the situation of each but the teacher was so knowledgeable and I feel my knowledge of Church History was greatly enriched. I certainly know more of the outcome of the early Church Councils and the growth of the Eastern and Western Church. He was a White Father who has been in the Holy Lands for 40 odd years. He had a deep feeling for the people and the many Churches that strive to live in peace and understanding in this land to which they have been part and often a cause of the troubles that still exist.

We are just moving out of our first stopping point. I am refreshed with a coffee and chocolate bar. Our guide has been fantastic giving an almost non stop commentary of the land we have passed through. Much of it we have travelled earlier with Jarad who was our desert guide. I was disappointed to bypass Jericho but it might be on the return trip. Not likely though as we come back along the Mediterranean Sea route. At Jericho the scene began to change and lush gardens appeared. Apparently the merchant Palestinians make it their winter home. When Jerusalem gets cold, even snow, they move down to this almost tropical climate.

We are now in such a vastly different area to the desert land surrounding Jerusalem. I had best listen to the continuous commentary. We are now looking at gum trees from Tasmania. Like the trees imported into Australia they absorb too much water for this dry land and so prevent other native plants from thriving. We have just passed the mountain where the first king of Israel, Saul, died in battle with his old enemy the Philistines. David grieved deeply for Saul and his son Jonathan and cursed the mountain so that nothing ever grew or was planted on it again. It is one of the few mountains in this area that remains bare. Even today the Government respects the event and does not allow anything to be planted there.

Next the mountain where Ahaz built his castle and his wicked wife Jezebel was thrown to her death. Oh what rich and wonderful stories we have. What a day! I have walked and walked and walked. We have been to 10.00 Mass at the beautiful church of the Annunciation. We had time to walk around the interior of the Church before Mass started and admired the many magnificent national paintings of the Mother of God.

This magnificent building is another contributed to by all nations of the world and each has sent their impression of Mary as Mother. The walls of the church are covered and other paintings spill over to cover the walls of the outside courtyard. I took almost all in but time ran out and I was called back to the bus. But after Mass we went down into the crypt where the actual event of the Annunciation is beautifully commemorated. Behind wrought iron gates is an altar with the inscription "Here the Word was made Flesh."

I find it a great delight to be able to say, "This is what I believe." I sat in silence in the silence and prayed for all those I had promised to remember. That was all we saw of Nazareth, the capital city of Galilee yet in the time of this young woman it is estimated there were about 100 people in the small village.

Now we continued to drive through countryside rich in produce. Fruit trees, gardens stretching for miles. Occasionally a dairy farm. The Jewish dairies are very modern and the cows do not get to roam about but are in limited holdings. The Arab cows fend for themselves and stray as far as possible to get the feed they require. Now sheep and goats appeared in larger herds but of course nothing like Australia. We were on our way to a recently excavated city of Zepphoris. It is reported to have been built by one of the Herods about the time of Jesus and there is much speculation as to whether Joseph and Jesus are men who were more than carpenters, came to work here.

It is a town not mentioned in the Gospel yet in those days would have been a relatively short walk across the fields from Nazareth. That part is not hard to explain as it was Herod's town built for himself and his Roman friends. Not a town where Jesus would have been welcomed or where he would have been inclined to go. We sat in the seat of an amphitheatre where dramas and music recitals would have taken place. We even had our own little recital with the talents we have as a group.

A synagogue has been almost restored and how things changed to accommodate the taste of the people there. Images of different characters are in the mosaics on the floor, all a far cry from Jewish Law. In another room which would have been the dining room of a wealthy Jew the beautiful mosaic which is called the Mona Lisa of the ancient world. A truly beautiful face. The paved mosaic streets have been uncovered.

Until recently an Arab village was all that was covering these treasures. When repairs had to be done to the village the treasures were unearthed so the villagers displaced. By now my feet were crying. I had walked far enough. Earlier we had had lunch at a tourist stop before starting the walk. Several of us now headed back there. We were then back in the bus heading for our final destination and central point for the following three days.

This is when I had my first glimpse of the Sea of Gallilee. Another very high point of my experience in this amazing land. A land of today with all its problems. A land of long ago with its rich and amazing story. On arrival most headed for a swim. I preferred a shower and a bed. As we leave tomorrow at 7.45 I feel it is time to end and get the energy that will demand. I shall remember you all wherever I go in these special days. Love now Helen

Monday, June 22, 2015

After a very satisfying breakfast we set out from our very restful and well equipped Guest House for the day's journey. We go first through Magdala and then a very modern Tiberius. For a while we drive along the Sea of Galilee and then turn inland and begin a climb up a very steep ascent. After a breathtaking drive up hairpin bend turns we have come to the very summit of the Golan Heights still known as the Disputed Territories. We stopped midway to see the natural boarder between the Kingdom of Jordan and Israel. There many scars and mementos of recent wars. Don't go off the road, we were warned, as land mines still exist.

At the top we come to a huge plateau stretching for miles. As the bus stops we have a magnificent panorama of the whole of the Sea of Galilee, looking the entire length and width. A magnificent indescribable view. We see where we came from and the towns of Magdala and Tiberius that we had driven through. We can see part of the cliff climbing road that had us so fearful.

We have been shown the very small area covered by Jesus. Yet we have come from all points of the earth to see and travel what I have read, learnt and taught so much about. Now I am on nearby hills looking down on his land. I am also looking at a land that is used for military and protective activities. The top of the Golan Heights is a huge plateau. After years of being just a defensive outpost it is now under extensive cultivation. Crops are in every stage of growth as the irrigation systems makes it a place of four seasons at once. Israel wanted the Golan Heights for security and water. Now she has found a third and productive use in agriculture. Field and crops all over this extensive piece of flat land. I just saw a unmanned drone take off!

We are in scary, anxious territory. Jews and Romans in Jesus' day. Jews and whoever today. After we have each had our fill of the view we thankfully get into the bus to return to what is proper Israel by another route. At the base of the mountain we make a right angle turn and are told we are back in the real land of Israel. From there we went to Cesare Philipi built by Herod's brother and named after the Roman Emperor and himself. Here we saw one of the three sources of the Jordan River and the place where Peter answered the question, "Who do you say I am."

Again we roamed around excavation of temples that came long before Jesus. Here too we saw our first native animal in a family of rock rabbits and then a startlingly green lizard who really performed for his audience. Down by the source of the Jordan we paused for lunch at a Lebanese restaurant. The owner is Lebanese but after some recent war the borders were changed so the man while still living in the same house, now lives in Lebanon but has his business in Israel. He and his family have to pass a check point twice a day coming to and going from work.

As we drove along we were continually reminded of recent destruction with bunkers built by both sides and tank destroyers built by Lebanon to try to stop the speed of Israel war machinery. There is an experimental site for wind farms and water storage under ground pumps scattered all over this rich source of water supply. Such a change after the limited water in Jerusalem.

Our next stop was the second source of the Jordan. A truly beautiful spot. Waterfalls in abundance. First to a quiet spot where we each decided just how immersed we would be to renew our Promises. I had taken my laplap from PNG so was prepared to go right in. I waded to the centre of the large pool where there was a tree surrounded by large rocks. I and my helper made it to there in almost freezing water and sat on the rocks. It was a moment of stillness in a busy day.

From there to see a real waterfall which meant down 100 roughly made steps. Paul was my supporter and guide going down and Agnes did it for the return. I find each one in the group so kind and considerate. The waterfall was worth the effort. There was a group of girls from an ultra conservative Jewish Secondary school visiting the site. They came up behind me and sang a song to urge me on. At the top they said Amen. I responded by singing the Amen from Sydney Poiter's 'Lilies of the Field'. They picked it up and we had a lovely time both singing and dancing. We were told later it echoed all over the parking area.

Our last stop was the fort of Dan, one of the 12 sons of Jacob. The excavations again amazing. Even down to the king or town leader's throne. We had an impromptu court session with a King who was pretty stern. All music and singing. A beautiful way to end the day. Very enjoyable. Lots of walking but not as strenuous as yesterday. We came home for a change then celebrated the Eucharist on the shore of the Sea of Galilee. A wonderful moment when the birds, trees and murmur of the waves added to the day.

Our guide, Carol Ann has given each a map and tonight marked in the route we have so far taken. Tomorrow we will add another line as we sail on the Sea of Galilee and celebrate Mass on the Mount of the Beatitudes. Each day becomes more amazing. Now to prepare for that day. My love to each as I remember you in prayer and joy Helen.

Tuesday, June 23, 2015

Truly I am lost in wonder. We have just had a beautiful boat trip, not sail, on the Sea of Galilee. In the middle of the Lake we stopped for a prayer and time of silence. I read the gospel of the calming of the sea from Luke. As we gently rocked I was back in Milne Bay. The scenery is so similar from one side of the lake to the other. I remember three special trips I had made when the engine failed and we rocked once in fiercely rough seas outside the reef at Rossell. Then I remembered I am here in another land with a magnificent lake that has changed so little in so many years. It was a peaceful, restful time.

We returned to shore and went shopping in the store where the boat is kept. What boat? I forgot we began the day in a kibbutz which houses a fishing boat excavated about 10 years ago. I remember seeing a documentary about 10 years ago on the ABC about its discovery? Here we saw a film strip which was most interesting about its discovery and restoration. They did not try to rebuild it but only preserve what was here and learn what they could from it. From there we went for the cruise on the Lake and then returned here for shopping. The shop really had some nice things so I did my first shopping in Galilee. There is so much to buy but two questions arise: How to get it home? And how practical and useful will it be?

Now we have moved on past the Church of the Multiplication of the Loaves and Fishes which remains shut following last week's vandalism. The police and insurance company are the only ones allowed in. Later in the day we will return to visit the five springs that are in the grounds which are still open. We are now at what could be Peter's mother in law's house. I am sitting in the church of Capernaum which is built above it.

The church has a glass floor so you can look down and see the remains of the house. The group has gone across to a neighbouring 4th century synagogue which is also coming to light after being hidden for hundreds of years. I feel my feet have carried me far enough for awhile and my eyes have seen enough ancient ruins. I shall save my energy for more important sites.

It is very hot here today but thankfully there is a pleasant cool breeze blowing. My friends return so I am off for a time. I have moved down by the Sea again and the wind has blown up. We were fortunate to have had our boat trip so early. It is incredible how similar the scene is to Milne Bay. I could be sitting at my first place there, Daio, and looking across to Alotau. But I am sitting at Capaneum looking across to Tiberius.

On another bus trip this time our lunch spot which is a Greek Orthodox Monastery. They took the order yesterday and today hand out freshly wrapped packages. There were just two choices so no great problem. On our way in we saw peacocks and then stood under the most twisted tree I have ever seen yet its branches spread out to form a glorious canopy. We walked under a vine covered archway to picnic tables again overlooking the Sea of Galilee. After lunch I visited their multi coloured chapel. The walls are covered with amazing icons many of which are impossible to understand without an interpreter which, in this case, we do not have.

Again the bus this time to the church of Peter's Supremacy. We had a short prayer in an outdoor chapel with a neighbouring group adding musical harmony to our gathering. Then down to the shore where it is believed Jesus met his apostles after the Resurrection and their return to Galilee. It is no wonder they returned when you compare Jerusalem with Galilee. The Desert and the Bread Basket of Israel. Which would you choose?

Standing at that shore, dipping my hands in the water, choosing a small stone the wonder of my faith came to me. I was overwhelmed with gratitude to Mum for that faith and all those who after her added to it. To believe is an amazing and wonderful thing. Then I went into the tiny church. In front of the altar is a huge stone with an inscription in Latin "Peter the Rock."

The final stop of the day the Mount of the Beatitudes. To get there, rather than turn back and go by Capernaum, we went north to the top of the Lake where it and the Jordan river become one. Somewhere close to where we were yesterday. We drove to the top of the highest hill on this side and looked across to the Golan Heights on the opposite side of the Sea. Magnificent views. Then a descent, all by bus thankfully, to the site of the Beatitudes. Where we had Mass again in an open air chapel. We have three great guitar players and a very musical man to lead us in singing. There is no way I can tell you what this has been like for me. Hopefully my tale gives you some idea of the wonder of it all.

At each stop there is the inevitable store. Always the

same things just different prices. I did any buying I still had at the first shop this morning. I am no great shopper so can walk and just look. Some of the group chose to walk home from here as the visit to the springs had been cancelled as the surroundings of the Church of the Loves and Fishes remains closed.

Tomorrow we leave after breakfast and return to Jerusalem. This visit has made me realise how true it must have been for Jesus "to set his face like flint towards Jerusalem" as Luke says. The scenery here. The beauty of the Sea of Galilee. The peacefulness of fishing. The rich lushness of the fields. The friendliness of the people. All left for the hustle and bustle of a big city, even in his days. The dust and dirt of the desert and for Him the unfriendliness of his enemies. We have lovely people to return to yet will be sad to say goodbye to Galilee. To each, signs from his land and love Helen

Tuesday, June 23, 2015 (later)

I am sitting quietly by the Sea of Galilee as the sun sets. It is refreshingly cool now and the sea is still again. The wind blew up strongly mid morning and we were counting our blessings that our boat trip had been our first port of call. Now as I am sitting here in the stillness and freshness of a cool breeze I am thinking of some of the wonderful poems I once read about things and place.

I think that I shall never see a poem as lovely as a tree. I love a sunburnt country. A land of sweeping plains. September the maid with the swift silver feet.

Did any poet ever write about this magnificent spot? The Gospel writers didn't really tell of its beauty just of its presence in the life of Jesus who must have found much joy in doing what I am doing and sitting at the lakeside at the end of a day or early in the morning as we shall do tomorrow with our last Mass here before we leave, at 6.oo. It is so beautiful. Love Helen

Wednesday, June 24, 2015

Well the last day in Galilee begins and will end in Jerusalem. I am thinking of how Jesus must have felt when he left Galilee for the last time? The freedom of fields and this beautiful Sea. To go to the dust and high walls because even in his time walls were part of Jerusalem.

WE ARE LEAVING Galilee and returning to Jerusalem via Cana. I am thinking of how Jesus must have felt as he left this land of open fields, fruit trees and the magnificent Sea for the dust, crowds and walls of Jerusalem. There were walls then as there are now. We began the day with a beautiful Mass down by the Sea as the sun rose through the trees. It was so peaceful and so easy to sing,"So I leave my boats behind." Our days are short now and this leaving reminds me that a final leaving and return will begin next Tuesday afternoon.

So we bypass Nazareth and Sepphoris which we visited on the way up to Galilee, and head towards Cana where Jesus turned water into wine for the wedding guests. Like the two churches at the Sea of Galilee, the Supremacy of Peter and the Beatitudes, this is a surprisingly small church. It has a massive entrance then inside is so gentle. Again we went to the depths of the earth to see what has been excavated under the church that proves how old it is.

This Cana however is not the Cana of Jesus time. That

was totally destroyed by the Romans in the year 70 when it defied Rome and refused to obey Caesar. That led to its disappearance. To keep the story alive a new Cana has been created to commemorate the famous event. The school of one of the principals travelling with the group is called "Cana Primary School." She had told the students she would be in Cana today. She told us the story of how her school had begun and received its name then read the Gospel of water into wine. As we walked out of the church we were handed a small glass of wine and a delicious "bird nest" cake. All a gift from her school.

We then set off for Caesarea on the Mediterranean Coast. We passed Mount Carmel on the way and I took the promised pictures. Hopefully they will mean something even though they only show houses on a hill. It is now both a farming and technological centre. And so we came to the Mediterranean Sea.

Can you believe it? I am standing on the sea shore as if I were standing on Coogee Beach. Truly I could burst like a multicoloured fire cracker! I only went paddling as it was an incoming tide, strong wind and a bit rough. If I had gone in someone would have been caring, worrying about me. Even paddling I could feel the drag under my feet and had to keep regaining my stance.

But before we got to the beach we went to some amazing places. After sitting in a fully reconstructed amphitheater we saw a film on the rise and fall of this great city. It was built by Herod the Great. Great mainly because he was such a fantastic builder - the temple in Jerusalem, the Citadel of David also in Jerusalem and this great Port City that began the trade between East and West that has never faltered even to today. I suppose he was " great" also for the other reason he is remembered - his brutality.

Even as the tide was receding we saw craftsmen working in the harbour excavating mosaic tiled floors. Herod held back the sea with great walls built around the city that extended into the sea. At his death the Romans took over then at a later date the Orthodox Church followed by the Turks, Crusaders and Muslims. Each left their mark of rebuilding or destruction. Then nature stepped in and an earthquake did what armies could not.

This time I did not mind the walking around investigating. It was on flat ground or up and down a reasonable number of steps. It was all so interesting after seeing the film at the beginning. We could even see the race track as in the great race scene in *Ben Hur*. Breathtaking. Can you wonder that I am bursting?

So lunch on the beach and swims and paddling for the faint hearted. Now we are in the bus and on the last leg of our journey to Jerusalem. It has been a beyond words experience. A gift of a lifetime. A gift for a life time. I have knowledge and images that will never fade. Our guide Carol Ann an American born Jew, our driver for four days Semea, a Palastin living in Jerusalem, have been fantastic companions. One has given us amazing facts, stories and spirituality; the other kept us safe on all manner of roads. All well sealed as the roads from north to south leave nothing to be desired. Now as we approach brown hills and fields as we move back to the south from the north I will stop and maybe add a closing sentence tonight after we arrive at Ecce Homo.

WELL WE ARE HERE HAVING BATTLED our way through the Arab part of the Muslim Quarter. It was time to be out buying for the evening meal after a day's fasting so the crowd was thick. One of the men, Barry, walked behind me to ensure a safe passage. I refused his offer to take my case until we turned the corner into Via Dolorosa. Then I asked him to pull it up the hill for me. Now an early night. I have just been invited to walk out for an ice cream but I fear I have had enough for one day. Again Blessings from this land and love Helen

ACKNOWLEDGMENTS

There are many people who have helped with the creation of this book. Thank you to the following:

Australia

Sister Ancilla White and Amanda McGreal at OLSH Convent for their help with photocopying and scanning.

Pam Tippett for perfect attendance at the Zoom meetings, despite her pneumonia, and her photographic contributions as well as her memories of Milne Bay.

Canada

Gillian Hutchings, Kristina Chandler, and Erin Hutchings for their help with transcribing, reviewing and suggesting.

Tim Goddard for photographs and reviewing the manuscript.

Victoria Goddard for designing the book.

Marilyn Myers for locating quotes when needed.

Elizabeth Watson for explaining the Rhesus Factor.

England

Virginia Weegenaar (Cook) for helping to transcribe and proofreading portions of the manuscript.

Evelyn Paterson for reading the manuscript for continuity.

United States

Candy Cochrane for helping to restore photographs.

www.ingramcontent.com/pod-product-compliance
Lightning Source LLC
Chambersburg PA
CBHW060356080526
44583CB00012B/346